THE ALLIGATOR'S LIFE HISTORY

The Alligator's Life History

Illustrated with Photographs
Taken by the Author

E.A. McILHENNY

Author of
"Befo' De War Spirituals," "Bird City," &
"The Wild Turkey and its Hunting"

Ten Speed Press

Ten Speed Press edition published September, 1987.

TEN SPEED PRESS
P O Box 7123
Berkley, California 94707

Cover Design by Brenton Beck

ISBN: 0-89815-230-5

Printed in the United States of America

1 2 3 4 5 — 91 90 89 88 87

The American Alligator, although very well known throughout the territory it inhabits, is a maligned and much misunderstood reptile, and but little accurate data has been recorded concerning it's life history. Owing to the location of my home, I have had unusual opportunities to observe alligators all of my life.

Avery Island, Louisiana, where I was born and have always lived, is a series of hills rising about two hundred feet above the coastal plain of South Louisiana and is located about half way between New Orleans and the Texas line. This happens to be about the centre of the greatest abundance of the Louisiana Alligators.

In my boyhood days before these reptiles had been disturbed by hide-hunters I came in contact with them constantly, and seeing them was such an every-day occurance that no unusual notice was taken of them by the children playing and swimming in the streams. They were looked upon as part of our natural surroundings, and we paid no more attention to them than we did to the flocks of birds about the place.

Our old family home, built in 1832 on the southwest side of Avery Island (which island covered about six thousand acres of hill and low land in its entirety, and has been the property of my family for several generations), stands upon a high hill which slopes down to the boat landing on the bayou, about five hundred yards from the house.

Among the earliest remembrance of my childhood is running down with my brothers and cousins and other small boys in the warm summer afternoons to the boathouse to swim; each boy trying to see who could get in the water first. The bayou is about one hundred and fifty feet wide

7

at this point and about ten feet in depth, with several shallow streams coming into it above and below the place where we swam. It is a tide-water stream and most of the time quite salty. In these days the alligators in the streams about the place were more than numerous, and of course, boy-like we always took great pleasure and not a little excitement in seeing how many 'gators we could call around us during our swim. We would attract them by imitating the barks and cries of dogs and by making loud popping noises with our lips, as these sounds seemed to arouse the 'gators' curiosity, and they would come swimming to us from all directions. We had no fear of them and would swim around the big fellows, dive under them and sometimes treat them with great disrespect by bringing handfuls of mud from the bottom and "chunking" it in their eyes. Sometimes when the tide was low we would surround on three sides a big one that might be lying on the edge of a flat, and create such a commotion splashing and jumping in the water that the alligator would crawl out on the mud-flat, and we would follow him "chunking" great handfuls of soft mud in his eyes and open mouth, and on several occasions in this manner we actually overpowered them, and after tying their jaws, dragged them to the house. More often when we would drive an alligator out on a mud-bank he would stand a certain amount of pelting with mud and then break through the circle of his tormentors to the water. Then it was, "boys get out of his way, he's going to the water." And you may be sure the boys scrambled. On one of these occasions I was pretty well mired past my knees in the soft mud and could not get out of the way and the old 'gator who was blinded with mud ran over me as I fell backward, and I still have the marks of his claws on my stomach, where he scratched me as he slid over my naked body. It was some time before I again ventured to bombard an alligator on a mud-flat.

Child-like, we had names for all the largest of the 'gators

and recognized them from year to year by some obvious peculiarity. I remember most especially old "Monsurat," easily recognized as the largest of our 'gator company, and one we never took liberties with. Monsurat was killed in the Fall of 1879 by our tutor fresh from Harvard, and hauled in triumph behind a four-mule cart to the house, and I remember seeing my father measure him eighteen feet, three inches, and hearing him say it was the largest alligator he had ever seen.

All this familiarity with alligators in my childhood did not "breed contempt" as familiarity so often does, but instilled in me a tremendous interest in these great reptiles that has remained alive through all my long life, and now as I near its close I will try to record some of the things I have learned concerning their life's history during more than three score years of living near to and observing them.

TABLE OF CONTENTS

11

TABLE OF ILLUSTRATIONS

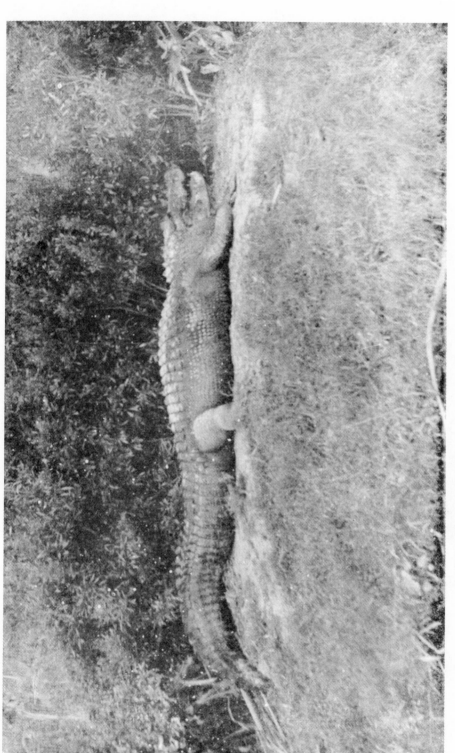

A TWELVE-FOOT MALE TAKING A SUN BATH ABOVE HIS DEN.

The Alligator's Life History

CHAPTER I

INTERESTING FACTS AND MIS-STATEMENTS ABOUT ALLIGATORS

The alligator with the exception of the crocodile of Southern Florida is by far the largest reptile inhabiting the United States.

Its general characteristics are too well known to need a detailed description in this book, the object of which is to deal more with its life history; which so far as my reading goes has never been truly told, although much literature has been published that in general is but a poor attempt of the authors to put into words things that if seen were not understood, or to record wild tales of illiterate hunters who were not true observers. I will, however, record for the casual reader, a few of the most interesting things of this great reptile's make-up.

The name "alligator" is undoubtedly a corruption of the name given it by the early Spanish settlers who were the first white people to visit and establish colonies along the Gulf Coast of North America. They, thinking it a giant lizard, called it *"el largato,"* meaning lizard. This was corrupted by the early settlers speaking English to *"lagato,"* which finally was changed to alligator, by which name it is known.

An alligator is a reptile having four short, rather weak, legs whose toes, widely spread, are joined almost to their tips by skin, which enables them to move more readily in water than on land, and helps them to walk without sink-

15

ing when coming out of the water onto the soft earth of the swamps and marshes in which they live. Their head is large, long and flat, with enormous jaws armed with long rows of formidable teeth, both top and bottom. Their necks are short and rigid. Their bodies are heavy, and about one-third the total length is between the front and back legs. The tail is long and heavy, tapering gradually from the hind legs to the end, being much thicker from top to bottom than from side to side, and is keeled on the upper side the last third of its length, which enables them to use it to great advantage when swimming. They propel themselves rapidly through the water by powerful sweeps of the tail from side to side. The legs and feet while swimming are folded back against the body and tail. An alligator's body, except the back of the neck and back, is covered with smooth horny scales in transverse rows, for the most part rectangular in shape, separated from each other and connected to each other by narrow bands of heavy, wrinkled, flexible skin. The back of the neck is covered with rather regular rows of heavy bone plates almost square, with rounded corners, and heavily keeled; these are set in the under skin, and provide a strong protective top armor.

The eye of the alligator is large. Its lens is a vertical slit, which is capable of being expanded or contracted as the light is bright or dull. In bright sunlight the slit is so narrow as to be hardly seen. As the light diminishes, the slit expands until after sundown, the pupil is almost round. The eye is protected by a top and bottom lid, both of which are movable, and which are closed when the alligator is asleep, either on land or under the water. The eye is further protected by a transparent membrane which slides across its lens from front to rear, and is closed as soon as the head of the alligator goes under water. The membrane remains covering the eye all the while the head is submerged. Alligators' eyes, as seen by a carbide or elec-

THIS BOY IS HOLDING CLOSED THE JAWS OF A NEWLY CAUGHT NINE-FOOT ALLIGATOR.

tric torch at night, are very brilliant and can be seen for a considerable distance, certainly four or five hundred feet. The eyes of the adult males shine red, and the eyes of the females and young a greenish or bluish yellow.

The opening of the ear is just back of the eye, quite large, crescent-shaped, and is covered by a flap of heavy skin hinged above. This ear cover is opened when the head is above the water and closed when the head is under the water.

The power of an alligator when closing its jaws and its power to keep its jaws closed is enormous. With a quick snap, it can crush the bones of a full-grown cow. I have an eleven foot alligator in my possession now, called Frank, who shortly after being caught had thrust between his gaping jaws a flat piece of two-inch-thick steel. He closed on this metal with such force, that the long ninth tooth on each side of his upper jaw was driven by the force of its closing on the metal clear through the bony top of his upper jaw, and the hollow ends of his teeth protruded above the bone. With an ordinary pair of heavy pliers, I caught hold of these teeth and pulled them through the jaw from the top, as they would never have grown back in place. The holes left healed over, but this alligator has never grown teeth where these were broken through.

If a large alligator closed its jaws, no man would have strength enough to open them, and I believe if a crowbar were used, the bone of the jaw would be broken before the muscles would give away; but any reasonably strong man, if he does not become frightened can hold closed the jaws of the largest alligator, with one hand, by catching the two closed jaws together at the snout.

There are two distinct types of alligators—one that grows long and slender, another that grows short and heavy. This fact is most noticeable in the males, and there is apparently no reason for it except a natural difference in stature. I have seen alligators twelve feet long that were certainly not more than twelve or fifteen years old, and alligators that were ten feet long that were certainly twenty-five years old. The age can be determined to a certain degree by the teeth, and by the ruggedness of the head. The older the alligator, the rougher the bone formation of the head and jaws, while a young alligator has rather smoother lines to both head and jaws. The teeth of a fully-matured alligator are almost solid all the way down, while an alligator that is not fully grown has hollow teeth, the top of which are dropped and replaced by new ones as its jaws become larger.

There is no difference in color between the male and female alligator. From an outward appearance, it is impossible to distinguish the male from the female in specimens under seven feet in length. Beyond that length, the male tends to become much thicker in body, and its head becomes much more rugged, and its jaws more powerful. Alligators are susceptible to change of color due to the water which they inhabit. The most brilliant colored alligators are found in the clear salt-water streams, and in the salt marshes bordering the Gulf Coast, where they do not come in contact with muddy or discolored water. The alligators having a yellowish cast to their skins are those inhabiting streams in which a great amount of drainage water flows. These are much lighter in color, with a decidedly yellowish cast, than are the alligators inhabiting the clean, salt water. The darkest alligators come from Tupelo Gum Swamps. The water in these swamps is almost black, being stained by the leaves, berries and roots of the Tupelo Gum. A small section of Tupelo Gum root, or a handful of Tupelo Gum leaves put into a bucket of water, will turn the water almost as black as if ink had been poured into it. Alligators inhabiting such waters are extremely dark in color. There is occasionally an Albino alligator. I had a skin brought to me that was entirely light yellow in color from head to tail. This skin was from a seven and one-half foot female alligator killed on Marsh Island in 1914 by Maxmillian Touchet. I have now a small alligator whose entire tail from its hind legs to the end is a light, lemon yellow. Very old alligators whether male or female lose to a large extent, the yellow stripes and blotches seen on the back and sides of immature specimens, and become almost solid black on back and sides. The yellow markings that are so prominent in the young being only faintly seen or being almost totally absent in the old. The underparts, however, remain through life a dusky yellow.

Alligators being reptiles are oviparous—that is, egg-laying. The eggs are a perfect ellipse and much longer than thick, and are covered with two protective layers. The outer hard shell is considerably thicker than that of a hen's, and is a glossy, clear white, coarse in texture, and very porous. The inner flexible membrane is tough and much thicker and stronger than that in a hen egg. There are no air chambers in an alligator's eggs as are found in those of birds. As soon as embryonic development begins, the central one-half of the egg becomes chalky white, while the one-fourth at each end remains clear. The albumen in an alligator's egg is much stiffer and more dense than in a hen's egg, and the color when fresh is a clear, pale, yellowish green. The yolk which is light yellow, is quite small in comparison to the size of the egg, and its substance is not nearly so stiff as that of the white. The embryo develops in the egg of an alligator about the same as the embryo develops in a chicken egg, and when ready to hatch the little alligator lies curled inside the egg with its back to the shell, its tail under its chin, and its nose, upper jaw and top of its head lying flat against a side of the egg, nose close to one end. In this position, by rubbing the top of its nose against the egg's envelope, the sharp point on top of its nose comes in contact with the inner embryo envelope, and opens a hole through it, enabling the little one to go free.   There are five fingers and four toes; the inside three of each member being provided with strong claws.

To quote all the published mis-statements concerning the life history of the alligator and correct them would require several volumes the size of this book and larger. I will, however, refer to a few of them, so that a small idea may be gained as to how this poor reptile has been maligned.

In writing of the nesting habits of alligators, Dr. Hugh M. Smith, in the Bulletin, United States Fish Com., XI, 1891, page 343, gives the following information:

"The maternal alligator in April or May seeks a sheltered spot on a bank and there builds a small mound. The foundation of the mound is of mud and grass, and on this she lays some eggs.   She covers the eggs with another stratum of grass and mud upon which she deposits some more eggs.   Thus she proceeds until she has laid from one hundred to two hundred eggs."

The facts are that the maternal alligator builds her nest complete before beginning to deposit her eggs.   All the eggs are laid at one continuous time, and not in layers.   No material is put between them.   The greatest number of eggs I have ever seen in the hundreds of nests I have opened was sixty-two (62), and the most ever reported to me was eighty-eight (88).

Dr. Smith in this same article further states:

"Unfortunately alligators grow very slowly.   At fifteen years of age they are only two feet long.   A twelve footer may be reasonably supposed to be seventy-five (75) years old."

The facts are that alligators grow at an average of about twelve inches a year up to a length of nine or ten feet in the males, and under normal conditions a two foot alligator

is not more than two years old, while a twelve foot alligator
would not be more than sixteen or twenty years old at the
most.

From "The Fur Animals of Louisiana"—Bulletin 18
(Revised), published by the Department of Conservation
of the State of Louisiana, January, 1931, we get the following remarkable information:

Page 174—"According to information gathered while
making surveys of the alligators of our State, it has been
ascertained that the alligators mate during the latter
part of February and the first of March."

The facts are, alligators mate in Louisiana from the
tenth of April until early June, never earlier and rarely
later.

Page 175—"The mating takes place on the ground."

The mating always takes place in the water.

Page 175—"Mating is accompanied by a great deal
of fighting on the part of each, slapping one another with
their long heavy tails; the cow using not only her
tail, but jaws, even if the attentions of the bull are not
distasteful."

I have witnessed the mating of alligators dozens of
times, and have never seen the cow show any desire to fight
her mate.   I have seen rival bulls fight during the mating
season.

Page 176—"The nesting site is in most instances a
dry piece of ground, sometimes an acre or two from the
hole."

As alligators live in marshes and swamps often many
miles from dry ground; "dry ground" is rarely used as a

nesting site.　The usual nesting site is wet marshes or swamps, and often in water several inches deep.

Page 178—"She carries the paillie fine, bulrush, three-cornered rush, cat-tail, saw grass, or other marsh vegetation in her mouth and piles it into a rounded heap from 18 to 20 inches high, and from 3 to 4 feet across.　This first layer completed, the first eggs are laid, and then grass is added and more eggs laid, until the nest reaches a height of 3 feet."

The nest is practically completed so far as height is concerned, before the eggs are laid.　The eggs are laid all at one continuous operation, and no grass is put between them.

Page 179—"One noteworthy thing reported by alligator hunters is that there are two color phases in Louisiana—black and yellow.　They seem to hatch in these colors and hold the phase almost to maturity and the two phases come from the same nest."

The different color between alligators is due to the water in which they live.　Those living in swamp water are always much darker than those from tide-water or the water of drainage streams.　The young from the same nest are always the same color.

Page 180—"Bullfrogs eat a great many."

How can a bullfrog, with a stomach of less than four inches, swallow even a day old alligator, whose length is at least eight inches!　Then the mother would make short work of any frog catching its young.

Page 180—"At the time they hatch, the alligators are from five to seven inches in length.　They grow from four to six inches the first year; in two years they are from sixteen to eighteen inches in length.　From three years and up they grow rapidly until they reach the

length of five feet; then they grow only about one and
one-half to two inches a year."

Alligators under normal conditions grow more than
twelve inches the first year, and the males about twelve
inches a year each succeeding year until nine or ten feet in
length.   The females maintain the same rate of growth
as the males up to seven feet.   After about seven feet in
length is reached the females grow more slowly, as their
maximum growth is about nine feet.   I have measured
hundreds of newly-hatched alligators and never saw one
less than eight inches in length.   They usually measure
nine inches and more.

> Page 184—"A pole, about seven or eight feet in
> length, of two-inch dressed pine with an iron hook at
> one end is used.   An alligator hole is found and the
> hunter proceeds to "feel" for the 'gator by sounding the
> ground around the hole to locate the cave.   If "felt"
> the hunter leaves the hole a short distance and calls the
> reptile by imitating its suckling cry of "umph, umph,
> umph."   As a rule, the 'gator responds and crawls out
> of the hole; if it is the size wanted, the hunter with a
> well-aimed throw of his hand axe, stuns the 'gator and
> with additional licks finishes it."

The alligator is no simpleton, and if a hunter punches
one with a hooked pole, you may be quite sure that alligator
will stay out of sight for several hours, in spite of the
hunter's "umphing"—then whoever saw an alligator
"suckling"?   A hunter who is skillful enough to stun an
alligator by a "throw of his hand axe" could find a far
more lucrative profession as an axethrower on the vaude-
ville stage.   Then, how much more efficient is a fifteen to
eighteen foot pole, the length really used for locating the
alligator to be "felt" way back in its den under the ground,
than one "seven or eight feet in length."   If the alligator
is "felt" it is prodded with the hook-end of the pole until

it bites the end, when the hook is fastened in some part of its mouth or throat, and the alligator pulled from its hole and killed by striking it on the head with the hand axe, not by throwing it.

CHAPTER II

Habitat, Dens and Hibernation

The habitat of the alligator in Louisiana was, until about thirty-five years ago, all the lowlands of the State. They were to be found in all considerable areas of fresh, brackish, and salt water marshes, and fresh water swamps from the Gulf to the State's northern border, and in years past were one of the most picturesque features of our lakes, rivers and bayous. They have, beginning about forty-five years ago, been hunted so relentlessly for their skins that they are now greatly reduced in numbers, and in many areas where they were formerly abundant, are now exterminated. Their natural habitat is water; and although they make long journeys over land, and can live for months without water, they are not happy away from it. In water they are quick and graceful and at home. On land they are heavy and awkward and can move only slowly. A child can walk faster than an alligator can run on land, but in the water they can move, for short distances, at least, with great speed, over-taking easily anything that swims, except the swiftest fish. They prefer shallow water to deep water, and in the overflow sections of the State they often pass their entire life away from any permanent body of water.

Many of the Louisiana swamps, which are covered with water for a few months by the annual spring rise of the Mississippi River and its tributaries are practically dry for the rest of the year. In such locations alligators dig considerable holes, sometimes four to six feet in depth and with surface openings ten feet or more across. These holes are connected with underground dens which they have dug out, sometimes as much as forty feet long; into which they retire on the approach of danger, and in which they spend the cold winter months. These dens are usually kept filled with water by the summer rains after the spring freshet recedes, or are dug to the water table which is never more than a few feet below the surface in the swamps and marshes. I have found these 'gator holes in the swamps, miles away from permanent water, with their occupants living apparently normal lives. I have found inhabiated alligator holes with openings not more than four feet across, but extending a considerable distance underground, a long way from any stream, in the great, wet coastal plains of Southwest Louisiana. Such holes when made in solid marsh or swamp would always have piled to one side a mound of silty clay, which must have been deposited in its position by the alligator's carrying it in its mouth, as such holes were too small and the ground too hard to allow the earth's having been moved by sweeping it from the hole by the alligator, with its tail—the usual procedure when dens are dug in soft ground.

During the Winter alligators are inactive and spend about five months, from early October to late March, in holes or dens which they have made and into which they retire during the cold weather. These dens may be under the bank of some stream or lake, or in a swamp or marsh at a considerable distance from open water. Their dens are always made in wet land or under a bank, bordering water, and, except in severest drought, are filled with water. As a rule, the same den is occupied by the same alligator during cold weather as long as it lives. I have known instances where large, old alligators who had their dens at small ponds in the marsh never to leave these ponds, relying for food on such animals, birds and reptiles as would come to the hole for water, or in search of food. Most alligators, however, spend only the cold weather at these dens; leaving them for some stream or other open water as soon as Summer begins, and on approach of cold weather going back to them for the Winter.

I have always been familiar with 'gator holes, and the underground dens that are used as a retreat during cold weather by all large alligators and by the female as a refuge for themselves and young during the first Winter and Spring after the young are hatched.

It has been my good fortune on a number of occasions to observe alligators while building their dens, or "holes" as they are commonly called.

The first time I ever saw an alligator at work on its den was in late September of 1894; I had gone out to shoot Blue-winged Teal, which were then quite plentiful in the shallow bayous and marshes surrounding Avery Island. The tide was running out, and as I paddled my pirogue up a stream known as Alligator Bayou, I noticed muddy water coming out of a small side bayou making in from the south bank; thinking that a flock of ducks were feeding in this stream and stirring up the mud, I paddled very cautiously up it, it being about twenty feet wide and with about eighteen inches of water in it. Each time I rounded a point I picked up my gun expecting to see ducks ahead. I proceeded in this way perhaps six or eight hundred feet, when on rounding a point I saw the water in commotion and swirling, about fifty feet ahead of me. I stopped my boat against the bank, not knowing what was causing this disturbance, but thought it was a school of large fish. As I watched I saw the back and tail of an alligator come to the surface, the tail waving slowly, but with great power from side to side, and then as I watched, it slowly disappeared into and under the marshy bank, and the commotion in the water ceased. I then realized that an alligator was digging a hole for its winter home. After the alligator had disappeared, I quietly paddled my boat into a little slough just below and almost opposite to where the alligator had gone under the bank, and waited developments. I could

see that there was some commotion going on in the hole
from the abundance of muddy water that was coming out
of it, and as the water was clear above the hole and the
tide running out, I knew that this alligator was the cause
of the muddy water I had noticed at the junction of the
small stream with Alligator Bayou. After watching for
eight or ten minutes, heavy muddy water started boiling
out of the hole, and in a little while I could see the end of
the alligator's tail as it backed from the hole, and on both
sides of the tail was a great mass of soft mud mixed with
grass roots. As the alligator's body backed out of the hole
I could see that it was pushing this material out with the
flat of its webbed hind feet. After backing its body a little
more than half way out of the hole, it disappeared again
under the bank and there was very little commotion for
about five or six minutes; when heavy muddy water began
to boil out of the hole as the alligator again backed out
pushing a considerable mass of loose material from the
hole with its hind feet. This time when its tail was half
way out of the hole it began waving slowly but strongly
from side to side, creating an eddy very much like that
created by a boat's propeller. This tail action completely
spread the mud that had been pushed out of the hole, mix-
ing it with the water which in turn carried it down stream.
I stayed, watching this work, for at least an hour, and during that time the alligator came entirely from the hole only
once. It was a large "bull" or male, at least twelve feet
long, and although I was within twenty feet of him, the
wind was favorable, and my boat being hidden by the overhanging grass which partly concealed me, he did not show
any suspicion that danger was near. I left quietly while
he was hidden, expecting to come back and catch him, but
I did not again visit the spot for several years, and then
found the hole filled up with silt and deserted; he had probably been killed by a hide-hunter.

1925 and 1926 were unusually dry years in Southern

Louisiana, and the marshes, ponds and considerable lakes became dry.   During this prolonged drought many alligators were forced to leave their dens and make new ones where they could find water.   In early September, 1926, one of my men trailed a very large alligator for a couple of miles through the dry swamp east of Avery Island, and found where it had gone into a small pool on the edge of the swamp that was kept filled with water by the tides.   My men always report to me any extra large alligator they happen to see; and because of the description of this one, which the man said was very large and only partly covered by the water and mud in the pool, I went at once to investigate.   Before we got to the pool we heard a considerable commotion of the water, and from the noise I surmised the alligator was deepening the pool for its winter den. Proceeding very quietly to a point from which the water was visible through the underbrush, I could see the back and tail of a very large alligator whose head was hidden under the bank, and whose tail was strongly sweeping from side to side. This little pond was not more than twenty-five feet across and about eighty feet long, and was completely surrounded by trees and had in it not more than ten inches of water. The alligator had not had time to be at work for more than three hours, as it had freshly arrived at the pond, and had not done any work when seen by my man earlier in the day, but when I arrived it had already cleared the mud and trash from a space about twelve feet wide by fourteen feet long, and had made it at least twelve inches deeper than the rest of the pond, sweeping the soft material and fallen branches from the bottom of the pool into considerable flats to each side of where it was working, and had torn a hole under the bank at least two feet back.   Although this alligator was very large, between thirteen and fourteen feet long, it was very poor, and I thought it would be better to leave it in its natural den all Winter and get it in the Spring, so we sat there and watched it work.   In excavating under the bank, it would tear the earth and roots loose with its mouth, and back out with great mouthfuls of this soggy material which it deposited clear of the bank in the water, and then brushed it aside with strong side waves of its tail. When large roots were encountered, they would be grasped with the jaws and the entire body jerked back until the roots were either bitten off or torn out. Such power was used in this root-breaking operation, that we could see the trees whose roots were being torn out shake to their very tops, and some of them were a foot or more through at the base. In this way roots eight or ten inches in circumference were removed. As the hole got deeper the loose material would be pushed back and out by the hind feet. I watched him at his work for about four hours, and by the end of that time only about two feet of his tail was sticking out from under the bank. I visited this den the next April and found the alligator had left, and I followed its trail to the end of Saline Bayou, and although he has been seen a number of times since, we have not been able to catch him. He is now in his old den located about two and a half miles back in the heavy cypress swamp east of Avery Island; a den so long and deep that it would require great effort to get him out of it. I have known of this alligator in this particular den for more than thirty years. He was a large 'gator when I first saw him.

The location of alligator holes or dens in an ordinary marsh or coastal prairie can be told from a considerable distance by the height and vigor of the growth of grass surrounding them. No matter whether it is bulrushes, saw grass or other water-loving grasses, the growth immediately around the alligator hole, especially near the part of the bank that it uses for pulling out in the sun, is very much more vigorous, and the grass greener and taller, probably due to their roots being fed by the droppings.

Sometimes large, old alligators have their dens in open shallow lakes or ponds, and do not go under the land to

THE DEN OF THIS ALLIGATOR IS JUST BACK OF AND UNDER IT.

spend the Winter. I have seen several of these open dens, and have fallen in a couple of them. I was hunting ducks about twenty years ago in what are known as the Deep Bayou marshes in South Central Vermilion Parish. These lands at that time belonged to the late Paul J. Rainey and to me. I had my decoys on Deep Lake, but the afternoon was warm and there was no wind, with but few birds moving my way. I noticed quite a steady flight of ducks in small bands lighting in the marsh about a quarter of a mile east of me, so I left my boat and walked across the marsh to find out what the ducks were doing. When I got near the spot at which they were lighting, I saw there were a great number of ducks in two small round ponds, each about two hundred feet across and divided from each other by a narrow strip of grass not more than twenty feet wide. I flushed the ducks without firing my gun, so as to frighten them as little as possible, as I knew, if not frightened, they would go to one of the large ponds in the vicinity and come back to these ponds in small flocks, affording splendid shooting. At a glance I saw the best place to stand for the incoming birds would be on the strip of grass between the two ponds. In order to get to it, I had either to walk around the nearest pond or wade across. As I knew all the ponds in this marsh were hard bottom and shallow, I started wading. The water was less than knee deep and the going good until I got almost half way across, then the bottom began to suddenly get soft, but thinking it was only a pot hole, I kept on, and in a few steps more was in slush up to my armpits. As I made another step I felt my foot strike something solid, and thinking it was the opposite side of the hole, raised my foot until I got something hard underneath and heaved myself up. I had just thought how nice it was to get out of the slush, when it seemed as if an earthquake had struck me, and my feet lost the bottom, the mud and water around me began to boil, I got a hard blow on one leg below the knee which I afterwards found was cut to the bone, and I was thrown

violently to one side and went under. Fortunately, I did
not lose my gun, and as soon as I could find my feet, lost
no time in getting to the grass. In spite of my shake-up,
I had very good shooting; but walked around the edges of
the ponds to pick up the ducks I shot, instead of crossing.
What happened was—a very large alligator had deepened
the centre of this little pond for his den, and when I stepped
on him, he threw me off his back and hit me on the leg with
the side of his jaw. I don't think for a minute he made
any attempt to catch me, for he could have easily done so.

There was another very large alligator whose den was
in a pond in exactly the same sort of a position as the one
I fell in, not more than a mile from this one, and for more
than fifteen years I offered a reward to the trappers who
worked these lands for the capture of these big fellows
alive, but they were so smart they could not be caught.
During the great drought of 1925-1926, these ponds dried
up, and both alligators disappeared and have never been
seen since. They probably went to open water and were
killed by hide-hunters.

During the winter months, occasionally alligators are
caught away from their dens, and on cold days become completely numbed, and incapable of moving. A rather amusing incident happened to me in connection with a numbed
alligator. One day in January, 1895, I was hunting Jacksnipe on the burned-over marshes west of Avery Island
with my friend, H. P. Kernochan of New York. The tide
was very low, with quite a stiff norther blowing. We
started hunting about nine o'clock in the morning, and
working backward and forward across the burns came to
a bayou about twenty-five or thirty feet wide, in which there
was very little water. Most of the snipe that we flushed
lit across this bayou, but as I knew the bayou had a soft
bottom, I did not feel like crossing. In going along its
border, I saw in the centre of the bayou an alligator perhaps nine or ten feet long. There was only about six or

eight inches of water covering it, and as the water was clear, its entire body was plainly seen. Harry wanted to kill it, as he had never shot an alligator, so fired a couple of loads of No. ten shot at its head as it lay under the water in full view. We cauld see the shot marks on the alligator's head, and we thought it had been killed, as it did not move. Later that day, having hunted out the snipe grounds on the side of the bayou we were on, I decided to cross and hunt the far side. I told Harry how to use his legs to keep from sinking too deep in the mud, and told him to go across first, so that I could give him assistance if he needed it. There was only about a foot and a half of water in the bayou, but I knew the mud was quite deep. Harry started across, but instead of spraddling and walking on his knees with his legs at as near right angles to his body as possible; he tried to step straight, and after a few steps was bogged down to his crotch. I told him not to struggle, that I would go down to where he had shot the alligator and push it up to him and he could use it as a pry to lift himself on. The alligator was only about twenty feet below us with the head pointed upstream to where Harry was. I, knowing how to walk the mud, had no fear of going into it and went in just about mid-way to the alligator. On reaching it, I put my hand on its hind leg and started shoving it towards Harry. The alligator immediately began taking steps and moving along in a very sluggish way. Meanwhile, I had told Harry to throw his gun and hunting coat onto the bank of the opposite side. When the alligator started crawling slowly towards him, I said to him: "You did not kill the 'gator, and he is coming to you as fast as he can." This frightened Harry very much, and in almost less time than it takes to write it, he had dug himself out of the mud and was flat on his stomach, going for the bank in exactly the same position that the alligator was in. When he finally got out, he was plastered with mud from the top of his head to his feet. His hat was gone, and he was a most ludic-

rous sight.   Fortunately, I had a large knife in my pocket
with which I could scrape him off, and as his gun and car-
tridges were dry, we continued our hunt, but he was a very
nervous individual, and I could not get him to cross the
bayou later in order to get to the boat; so he followed its
bank to the main bayou and I crossed, got the boat, and
joined him.   This alligator was completely numbed by the
cold, and was too far under water for the light load of bird-
shot to do it any damage.

For many years I have kept several unusually large
alligators in pens, built on the edge of the pond which
covers most of my Bird City (egret colony) only a few
hundred feet from my house.   In one pen about thirty feet
square I kept a big fellow almost twelve feet long who, on
account of his age and size, I called Grandpa.   Under
date of September 6, 1924, I find the following entry in
my alligator notes:

"I have been much interested in watching Grandpa
deepen and enlarge his winter quarters.   The water in the
pond is very low, as we have had no rain for several
months, and the old boy has not had enough water to cover
his back for some days.   Yesterday he commenced deepening and enlarging his den, and deepening the hole in front
of it.   He began by putting his head and shoulders in his
den and sweeping with powerful side strokes of his tail, all
the soft material from the bottom in front of it.   The soft
mud was only about three inches deep, and when that was
out of the way, his back was not yet covered with water.
He then felt the place he wanted to deepen over, by pushing his nose hard over every part of it.   He then lined up
with the opening of his den where it goes under the bank,
and began scratching up the bottom with his hind feet.   In
order to hold himself in position for digging with his hind
feet, he braced his head and front feet on the bottom, pushing back hard, at the same time bringing up one hind foot
after the other, driving them back slowly, and with all his

power digging the claws of his hind feet into the hard clay
of the bottom, and stirring it up as much as possible.
When he got a spot worked up, he moved forward or back
a step and went through the same performance.   When
he got a strip of bottom five or six feet long and half as
wide softened, he went forward until his tail was over the
soft spot, when with slow powerful sweeps of his tail, he
quickly moved the soft earth to the sides and away from
the part he was deepening, down to hard ground.   He continued these maneuvers back and forward until he had
made a hole about three feet deep and ten feet long and
built up a mud bank several inches high on each side of it.
He is now deepening his den where it goes under the bank.
In working in his den he evidently loosens the earth with
his claws both front and back, and pushes it out with the
flat of his big hind feet, and after getting the loose material outside the den, he sweeps it from the hole he has dug
with side strokes of his tail.   He does not use his jaws in
bringing the earth from his den as is popularly supposed."

When alligators were still plentiful in the lowlands of
Louisiana, all heads of bayous, marsh ponds and swamp
water holes had leading to them, from one another and
from the larger streams, distinct trails which were known
to the settlers as "alligator roads."   These trails were
usually about three feet wide, fairly straight, and all
vegetation in them was kept mashed down by the dragging
of the bodies of these heavy reptiles over them.

Alligators are great travelers in a local sense, and for
no reason which a human being understands will desert a
certain locality, going overland considerable distances to
other ponds or streams.   There are on Avery Island, a
number of artificial ponds formed by damming the valleys
between the hills.   Some of these ponds contain as much
as fifty acres of water, and some of them very much less.
These ponds are all located from one to two miles—possibly a little further—from the lowlands, and are sepa-

rated from the lowlands by timbered ridges exceeding one hundred feet in height.   In every one of these ponds, every Summer, alligators appear and remain for a short time, as suits their pleasure, and as suddenly disappear.   I have frequently found them traveling long distances from water, both on the prairies and in the wooded hills.   My house is located on a hill one hundred and fifty feet above tide level, and a little more than one-half a mile from the marshes which lie to the west.   Directly east of my house, about one-quarter of a mile, is a considerable artificial pond that was first dammed in 1892.   I have a number of times found alligators in my grounds within a hundred feet of the house on their way from the marshes to this pond. There are in this pond a number of alligators that are in sight every day of the summer.   One is an especially heavy male that is upwards of ten feet in length.   This alligator left the pond during the last days of May, 1933, and re- turned to the pond August sixth.   His trail was seen going out, and his trail was seen returning, as both times he passed directly through my flower garden.   Why he made this journey to the marshes and back again is a mystery, for the pond teems with all kinds of food that alligators love, and the mating season had about passed when he went out.

In one of the other ponds on the place was a very large male alligator that measured between eleven and twelve feet, who came into the pond the year after it was built from at least a mile and a half away, as there is no bayou or swamp where he could have lived in a less distance.   This alligator built a den under the bank of this pond and spent the Winter there.   The next Spring he left the pond in April and went to the swamp to the east, his trail being plainly seen.   He returned in early October, wintered in his den, left the pond again about the middle of the next April and continued going and coming to and from the pond for five or six years, always going out in April and coming back in early October and spending the Winter in the den he had dug in the hard ground under the bank of the pond. One Fall he failed to come back, and he has never been seen since, and as I did not hear his voice, I supposed he wandered into some of the streams and was killed by a hide-hunter.

Rather an amusing thing happened on one occasion when quite a number of Bohemian immigrants who had newly arrived at New Orleans came to my place to work. Eight or ten of the men were sent out to the corn fields to break corn in the early Fall. They returned a few minutes after getting to the field, very much excited, gesticulating, and all talking at once. As their interpreter was not around, they were brought to me, and I tried to find out what the trouble was. None of them could speak a word of English, but all of them tried to show by pantomine what was causing the excitement. They would make short jumps, puff themselves up, and blow a hissing sound through their mouths. I thought they had seen a snake, until one of the men lay down on the ground on his stomach, swelled himself up as much as he could, stretched his two arms full length in front, putting one on top of the other, then opening them from the hand to the elbow, made at the same time a loud hissing sound, and tried to wiggle along the ground. The imitation was so good, that I understood at once that they had seen an alligator. Accompanying them to the field, they showed me with a great exhibition of fear where the terrible thing they had tried to describe had been. I could see the trail of a large alligator, and following it for a few hundred feet found it in the corn rows, but as it was rather a small one—only about ten feet long, I did not molest it, and let it go on about its business.

Old alligators usually inhabit the same den year after year, enlarging it from time to time until it becomes quite a labyrinth under the ground. They retire to these dens in October and invariably spend the entire Winter in them or on the bank of the den. Alligators in this climate do not hibernate for any great period. They go into winter quarters, as it were, early in October and at that time cease taking food of any kind. They keep in their dens in cold weather; that is, when the air is colder than the water. When the air is warmer than the water, they come out of their dens and spend the bright part of the day on the bank in the sun, and even if the sun is not shining, if the air is warmer than the water, they spend considerable time on the bank. They do not, however, move away from their dens until the last days of March or early April, and an old alligator will not take food from the time it goes into its den until it leaves it.

It is generally supposed, and is so stated by writers who have described this phase of the alligator's life, that during hibernation they stay buried in the mud. This however, is not a fact. Alligators who have built wintering places underground have at some point in their dens, one or more small holes opened through to the surface. In these small openings, which may be only a few inches across, they poke their noses at irregular intervals in order to get fresh air. No matter what the temperature is outside, an alligator always puts his nose to the surface to breathe, and does not remain completely dormant for any great length of time. Sometimes an alligator's den—especially in soft ground—will be as much as forty to sixty feet long or longer, with one or more branches and outlets. These are dens that have been dug by large old individuals who seem to be especially weary and make their dens of this size in order to have more than one exit in case they wish to get out without using the main exit.

Before the alligators were destroyed to any large extent, in the tide-water streams of Louisiana, anyone going along a stream near the bank when the tide was very low could see the openings to alligators' dens dug under the banks of the streams, as the tops of the openings of the dens are

THAT ALLIGATORS DO NOT FEED IN THE WINTER IS ILLUSTRATED BY THIS PICTURE TAKEN IN JANUARY, 1912. EACH DOT IS THE HEAD OF A SIX OR SEVEN INCH CATFISH (RISING FOR AIR) THAT HAVE COME TO THIS ALLIGATOR'S "HOLE" IN THE COLD WEATHER BECAUSE THE WATER IS DEEP AND WARM.

usually only about one and one-half to two feet under the top of the ground. By the size of the opening it can be usually determined something of the size of the alligator inhabiting the den. As a rule, alligators do not use their dens during the Summer, leaving them for the more open waters, but return to the vicinity of the den as cold weather approaches, staying at the den from the early days of October until Winter has passed. This does not apply to females with young, as they stay at their dens with their young from the time of hatching until the next Spring.

Alligators are very susceptible to changes of temperature, and for that reason they crawl out of the dens onto the banks when the air is warmer than the water, and for that reason they do not go upon the bank in Summer during the daytime when the sunlight is hotter than the water. In summertime it is a rare thing to see an alligator on the bank during the heat of the day, and they do most of their overland traveling at night.

CHAPTER III

Food

In discussing their food it must be remembered that alligators are inactive for fully five months in the year, and as a rule do not take food of any kind during the cold months, from early October to late March. Although they do not hibernate all this time, they keep pretty closely to their dens; coming out to take sun baths, only on bright days when the air is warmer than the water. During the summer months they are heavy feeders, and towards the end of Summer they store in their bodies quantities of fat which sustains them during the cold, inactive months. Occasionally alligators will take food as early as the middle of March, but this is unusual, and the usual time they begin feeding is about the first of April.

Following Summers that have been exceptionally dry, causing a shortage of food, and therefore a lack of opportunity to store fat for the Winter, alligators will start taking food in early March, if the weather is not too cold, but such early feeding is entirely irregular. There does not seem to be available any data covering the food of alligators from a wide portion of their range. Remington Kellog, Techinical Bulletin No. 147, United States Department of Agriculture, classifies the contents of the stomach of one hundred and fifty-seven alligators, but as one hundred and forty-six of these were taken in the tidal marshes of Louisiana, and the stomach contents would indicate from the bayous, it is to be expected that the contents of these stomachs would consist of the life most plentiful in tidal marsh-bayous. If an examination had been made of the food of alligators taken ten or more miles farther inland or above the tide flow or from the small ponds and

THIS PORTRAIT OF THE HEAD OF THIS TWELVE-FOOT ALLIGATOR SHOWS
THE HEAVY MUSCULAR DEVELOPMENT THAT OPERATES THE JAWS.

water holes away from the bayous, an entirely different menu would have been found.

It is quite safe to say that the food of the alligator at some period of its life, consists of every living thing coming in range of its jaws that flies, walks, swims, or crawls that is small enough for them to kill, and covers a tremendously wide range. In their young days, shortly after leaving the nest, their principal food is insects and small fish; after reaching a length of sixteen to twenty inches their food consists of crawfish, crabs, small fish, small frogs and other small reptiles and insects. After they reach three feet in length and larger, any creature inhabiting the land or water which they can catch and swallow is good food. Until they reach a length of five feet they are not a considerable menace to animals and the larger birds, although I have seen muskrats, rabbits, young ducks, rail and other small birds taken from alligators between three and five feet in length, but up to this size their principal food consists of small things.

Illustrative of how distructive small alligators sometimes are, I will give a couple of instances that have come under my personal observation:

On April 8, 1916, I was watching an old hen Dusky Duck with a brood of eight young ones swimming in the canal near my shooting camp in Vermilion Parish. The tide was low and the old duck had brought her newly-hatched brood to the water, and was quietly feeding with them along the edge of the canal, whose bank was steep and several feet above the water. I saw a small alligator swimming towards the old duck and her brood; when it got near it quickened its pace, and although the old duck flapped madly away, calling to her brood, who swam after her as fast as they could, the alligator overtook the rear young, grabbed one and throwing its head into the air, swallowed it, and with hardly a pause, swam rapidly after the others. In a distance less than two hundred feet it overtook, caught and swallowed one after the other all of these little ducks.   This alligator was not more than three and a half feet long.

On June 26, 1933, I, with a couple of my men, had been in the swamp to the east of Avery Island inspecting some canal work and dams.   While standing on one of the dams a King-rail and eleven quarter-grown young ones were seen feeding on the east bank of the canal not more than eighty feet from where we stood.   The old rail started swimming across the canal, followed scatteringly by her brood.   When the old bird and the first young were about half way over, a four foot alligator swam out from the shadow of the opposite bank, headed for the swimming birds.   I saw it almost as soon as it left the bank, and it almost immediately submerged.   The old rail also saw it and warned her young, with the rail's rattling alarm call.   All the young ones turned back, except one who tried to make the opposite bank with its mother.   Suddenly the alligator rose to the surface very near the swimming young rail and with a quick side snap, caught and swallowed it.   It then remained in the centre of the canal with only its eyes showing.   The mother rail was now on the opposite side of the canal from her brood, scolding and calling in an excited voice.   In a few minutes, three of the young rails started swimming to their mother.   They had hardly left the bank when the alligator submerged, and in a few moments came up alongside one of the swimming birds, caught it by a side swing of its head, swallowed it at one gulp, then swam rapidly after the other two, caught up with them just before they got to the bank where the mother rail was, and snapped up another; the third got safely to the shore.   The alligator then rested quietly with only its eyes showing.   The old rail had gone a little way up the canal bank and began calling to her young.   Four more of them started across, this time about twenty-five feet up the canal from the alligator.   On seeing the little rails in the water the alligator submerged, and in an incredibly short time came up along-side one of them, caught one with a side swing of its head, swallowed it and chased the other three to shore, without, however, catching another.   It must have known that there were more of the young rails on the opposite bank, for it kept very still with only its eyes showing above the water. In a very few minutes one of the other young started across the canal to join its mother.   The alligator on seeing it in the water submerged and came up alongside it, catching it in the same manner it had the others.   The remaining two met with the same fate.   What interested me more than anything else in watching this episode was the accuracy with which the alligator judged the distance in rising to the sur-face for its victims.   Each time it rose in exactly the right spot to catch the swimming bird with a side swing of its head, and these swings were made with flash-like rapidity. No attempt was made to catch any of the little rails from under the water, but the alligator rose to the surface each time before making its kill.   I believe, however, it could see the swimming birds while still below the surface.

Alligators that inhabit marshy pools in muskrat terri-tory live very largely on muskrats.   This I proved in 1916 while supervising the Louisiana State, the Sage and the Rockerfeller wild life refuges in the coastal parishes of Iberia, Vermilion and Cameron.   I had forbidden the kill-ing of alligators on these wild life refuges for four years, and they had become very numerous.   The men who trapped the muskrats on these refuges complained that the alligators destroyed a great many of the rats; so in April, 1916, I caused fifty alligators to be taken from the inland part of each of these refuges and had my chief warden examine the stomach of these alligators.   None of these alligators were killed in bayou or open water, all of them being taken from land-locked small ponds.   Muskrats proved to be the principal food of every one of these alli-gators, with an occasional gallinule, rail, duck, fish, rabbit and quite a number of snakes, but their stomach contents showed that muskrats predominated as their food. The stomach of one six-footer contained one mink, five muskrats. Another six-footer contained one rabbit, one rail and four muskrats. Many of these alligators were four to five feet long and some of them were over ten feet long, but all of them had been feeding on muskrats. Alligators taken in the bayous, canals and large lakes of these refuges a few weeks after this test, had been feeding entirely on fish, crabs and snakes, with an occasional rabbit, or bird, and only in one was a muskrat found; showing that the food of alligators depends largely on the location from which the reptile is taken.

I think the great increase in garfish in the inland waters of Louisiana is due entirely to the alligator having been practically exterminated in the bayous and small streams. I think, also, that the large increase of dusky-ducks, rails and muskrats in Louisiana marshes is due to the extermination of the alligator.

Wherever alligators are abundant there will be a great scarcity of all varieties of water snakes. I have seen wooded ponds on Avery Island in which there were no alligators, swarming with a number of variety of water snakes. Alligators would come into the ponds from outside marshes and in a comparatively short time no snakes could be found in or around the pond. I have seen comparatively small alligators, from four to six feet long, catch water snakes that weighed several pounds, and with a few crunches of the jaw kill them, then shift the snake until it was grasped by the head when it would be swallowed whole.

Alligators seem to know the difference between poisonous snakes and non-poisonous snakes. When an alligator catches a cotton-mouth moccasin, which is a poisonous snake, as soon as the snake is grasped in its mouth it is shaken vigorously until quite dead. This shaking makes it impossible for the snake to bite the alligator, possibly in the eye, which would be the only place on an alligator's head a snake's fangs could penetrate. When a non-poisonous snake is caught it is not shaken, but killed by being crushed between the jaws. I have seen alligators catch large terrapin and turtles of considerable size and crush their hard shells as if they were made of paper, swallowing them whole.

When an alligator catches food that is too large to be swallowed with its mouth closed, it raises its head above the water, and after pulping the food by numerous crushings between its jaws it is deftly shifted by throwing the object into the air until the head part points down its throat, when the whole object is swallowed at one gulp. Should the object be too large for the throat, and fail to pass in, it is ejected and again crushed between the jaws until it becomes more pliable, and then swallowed. I have seen a large captive alligator fed, at times, the shoulder containing the bone, and the backbone in sections as much as two feet long of full grown cattle, and these bones were crushed between the alligator's jaws as matches would be between the fingers of a man.

The crushing power of an alligator's jaws is enormous, and the muscular development operating the under jaw is tremendously heavy and strong. When even a three-foot alligator closes its jaws on an object it is impossible for a man with ordinary strength to open these jaws. When a large alligator closes its jaws on a victim, it is absolutely impossible, no matter what the strength of the thing grasped, for it to get away. This is the closing power of an alligator's jaws.

The opening power is exceedingly small. I have held closed with my left hand the jaws of the largest alligators I have ever caught. When handling alligators, even the largest, if it is on land, I usually press the top jaw down with a stick, grasp the top and bottom jaw at the nose with my left hand, and with my right pass a strong cord or rope around its jaws, and with a couple of half hitches the alligator is entirely harmless, providing one keeps out of the way of its tail.

When an alligator catches a large animal that is too large to be killed by crushing it in its jaws, it immediately starts rolling. The roll is accomplished by throwing its tail up and sidewise and turning its body at the same time and in the same direction that it twists its tail, holding its feet folded backwards against its sides; this twisting and rolling is done with great power, and the animal grasped in its jaws is violently thrashed about until it is quite dead. If an alligator catches an animal that is too large to be swallowed whole, it crushes the leg bones close to the body in its powerful jaws, and then by twisting, rolling and shaking, tears the member loose from the body when it can be easily swallowed. It is generally supposed alligators will not swallow food under the water; this is a mistake, however, as I have often seen alligators catch birds, fish and small animals and sink with them, swallowing the food while under the water. My observations are that an alligator can and will swallow while under water, food small enough to be swallowed without opening its mouth. If the food must be chewed, which necessitates opening its jaws, the head is always raised above the water. I have, on numerous occasions, when fishing on the bottom for large salt-water fish, using large baits, either fish or crab, had alligators swallow bait and hook, and for a few minutes they put up a hard fight when hooked on a fish line. That alligators sometimes hunt their food on the bottom of streams and ponds has been proven to me by seeing alligators that had not before been in view, rise to the surface with large water snakes, turtles or crabs in their mouths, which were killed and swallowed above the water's surface.

An examination of a number of alligators taken in the central part of the State, from above the tide flow, contained only fish, snakes and turtles, and in one instance an extra large one taken in the swamps of the Red River had swallowed a 'coon. I have never known of but one authentic instance of an alligator willfully attacking a human being unprovoked. I have known of several people who were supposedly drowned or bitten by alligators in the water, but on following up the cases I have proven everyone of them to have been attacks by large alligator-garfish.

Female alligators will attack man to protect their nests and young, but their movements on land are so slow, that there is no trouble in avoiding them, and in the water, they always give warning if they are about to attack by hissing and guttural grunts; giving a person ample opportunity to get out of their way. It is a wonder more men are not injured by these powerful reptiles, for those who make a business of hunting them for their skins are most careless in handling them; but it is a rare thing for any one to be hurt by an alligator.

I once saw an alligator about four and a half feet long catch one of my hounds by the side of the head as it was swimming a bayou on the east side of Avery Island after a wounded buck, and it came near drowning the dog. It twisted and tugged at the dog's head with such power as to pull the dog under the water causing it to lose its sense of direction and to become so fatigued, I am sure it would have been drowned had I not gone in the water and taking the alligator by the neck, killed it with my hunting knife. On another occasion a five foot alligator caught by the side of his head one of my bear hounds, Bull (who was an unusually large and powerful dog, but old), as he was drinking water from the bank of a pond near my house and drowned him. No one saw the alligator pull Bull in, but he was found in the pond dead, and a five foot two inch alligator, which I shot, watching his carcass. The side of his head and ear was badly lacerated by the alligator's teeth.

On another occasion I was shooting teal ducks in a long,

narrow, shallow, swampy pond early in April, and had one of my retrievers with me.   She swam across the pond after a wounded duck, and was pulled under the water by an eight to nine foot alligator.   The pond had never at that time been visited by aligator hunters and the place swarmed with the reptiles.   As it was one of my favorite places to hunt ducks, I re-visited it the day after my retriever was drowned; took a twenty-two rifle, sat on a log on the central edge of one side of this pond, and killed more than eighty alligators in a few hours, by calling them to me.   At one time there were more than thirty of these reptiles within one hundred feet of me, and those not shot at, paid not the slightest attention to the crack of the rifle.

The usual food of alligators from five to ten feet in length is fish of various kinds (preferably garfish), snakes, turtles and any kind of bird that comes in range of their jaws, and any kind of small mammal that they can catch. Muskrats, rabbits, coots, rails, duck, garfish, snakes and turtles form the bulk of the food of the larger size alligators.   In procuring their food they lie in wait on the edge of some stream or at a water hole, and anything swimming near them is quickly caught by swift side swings of the head with the jaws half opened.   If they see an animal swimming, they catch it with a remarkable burst of speed that is very much swifter than can be made by any mammal in water.

I have seen alligators catch various animals in water, especially rabbits and muskrats, and on a number of occasions, I have seen them catch hogs and once a 'coon.   Each time they approached the swimming animal with a dash of wonderful speed, and on grasping it in their jaws immediately sank under the water.   On one occasion I saw a duroc boar hog that weighed not less than five hundred pounds caught by a large alligator while the hog was swimming across a stream about eighty feet wide.   The hog had a regular crossing place at this point, and the alligator was waiting for him. As the swimming hog reached the middle of the stream the alligator, which had been hidden by the overhanging vegetation of the opposite bank, swam out with great speed, caught the hog at the shoulder, threw its tail almost completely out of the water and with a tremendous sweep to one side threw all four of the hog's legs clear above the water as it rolled over, and that was the last time I saw the hog alive. The next day its mutilated carcass came to the surface with all of its stomach torn out and one hind leg completely torn off. I had one of my men watch for this alligator, and on the third day he sighted it; got a shot and killed it. It was a very old alligator, its age being clearly shown by its badly worn teeth and the roughness of its jaws. It measured eleven feet seven inches with what was considered two feet to two and a half feet of its tail missing, and measured seventy-eight inches around the largest part of its body.

On another occasion a friend of mine on Bayou Vermilion saw an alligator catch a fat hog that was wallowing in shallow water on the edge of the bayou. This hog weighed approximately four hundred pounds, and it was terribly mutilated by the alligator, but not completely killed, as my friend got in a lucky shot which badly wounded the alligator, causing it to turn the hog loose. It was necessary to butcher the hog in order to save the meat, as it would have died from the wounds. The wounded alligator crawled out on the bank and was killed the next day. It measured a little more than ten feet in length.

In 1895, I was, early in April, shooting Jacksnipe on the cattle range west of Avery Island, and witnessed the killing of a three year old cow by an alligator. A number of cattle-men were driving a herd of cattle from the high range along the coast to a high range inland. In order to get from one range to the other the cattle had to cross a low marsh four miles wide. From many years of using the same trail a water-road had been plowed out by the animals across this lowland that was perhaps twelve feet wide and four feet deep, and it was through this canal that the cattle were obliged to swim this day.   As I stood talking to the owner of the cattle, Emile Thibodaux, on the side of this water-road, suddenly the leading cattle stopped and began to flounder trying to get out onto the marsh, then turned and started swimming back the way they had come. The herd was greatly excited and milled about considerably, and at last all of them turned back.   About two hundred yards from where we stood we could see a great commotion in the water, and thought at first that several animals had piled on top of each other and were bogged in the soft ground bordering the canal, as there was a great splashing and floundering in the water.   Suddenly the tail of a large alligator went up high in the air, we knew then the reason for the commotion was an attack on the cattle by an alligator.   I being on foot hurried across the boggy ground to the scene of the encounter, and as I neared the spot I could see the alligator rolling and twisting in its endeavor to keep a cow it had seized under the water.   When I finally got to the animals the alligator had killed the cow and had it firmly grasped by the thigh.   I shot the alligator with a load of number ten shot at a distance of about six feet, killing it instantly.   A number of the cattle-men having come up, we put a rope around its neck and pulled him out on the bank.   He measured ten feet, ten inches, and had a piece, perhaps two and a half to three feet long, missing from its tail.   We pulled the cow out and found it had been killed by drowning, and that the alligator had dislocated its thigh, and its teeth had torn through skin and flesh to the bone.   During this encounter, the alligator had thrown off such a quantity of musk that the water and bank was strongly scented with it.   The cattle-men tried several times to force the herd past this spot in the water-road, but it was useless, as they would not pass, and the drive ended in failure that day.   I was told later, that the next day in order to get the cattle through this part of the water-road some of the men were obliged to swim their horses ahead and the cattle then followed.

In April, 1905, I was standing on the wharf at the canning factory at Avery Island, talking to the night watchman just at dusk, when a large alligator appeared in the canal about fifty yards away. The watchman said: "I believe that is the alligator I have seen catch hogs as they swim across the bayou." I took the watchman's pistol (an officer's model 45 colt), and was lucky enough to put the first bullet just back of the alligator's eye and through the brain. It rolled over in the water throwing its two front feet in the air (a position always taken by an alligator when killed by a brain shot), dead. I sent a couple of men in a skiff to bring it ashore, and after skinning, it was found to have inside three pigs weighing about thirty pounds each that had been swallowed whole. This alligator was not quite twelve feet long.

On September 6, 1931, I was riding with my overseer, Nathan Foreman, through the woods on the south side of Avery Island and heard a thrashing and floundering in a swampy pond some little distance from us. We thought a cow had gotten bogged, and hitched our horses, going as quickly as possible towards where we heard the sound. The noise had ceased before we got off our horses, but as we had taken note of the direction, we hurriedly followed the line, and soon came to a spot at the edge of the pond where the water was stirred up, covered with bubbles and the bushes and growth on the bank were mashed and muddy. The tracks of a large deer and of a large alligator were very plain, and anyone could read by the signs what had happened. The deer had gone to the water to drink, and an alligator had caught it by one front leg and rolled with it until the deer had become exhausted, and had then pulled it under the water. In July, 1933, I killed this alligator; it measured nine feet, two inches, and had in its stomach the remnants of a 'coon, two turtles and two snakes.

These instances are proof enough that alligators kill very large mammals for food. I have never known of, or heard of an authentic case of a human being having been killed by an alligator, but I have known of several persons being quite badly bitten by alligators, because they were careless when catching them.

How quick an alligator can snap its jaws, was proven to me during the Spring of 1933. One Sunday afternoon I was walking with Doctor and Mrs. Crawford through my gardens when we came across a seven foot female alligator that had gotten out of its pen. Wishing to put it back, I picked up a small stick which I put on its top jaw pressing it closed. Holding the stick with my left hand, I reached with my right to catch the alligator by its two jaws so that I could tie them and then put it in the pen where it belonged. I was a bit careless and did not keep my hand in front of the alligator's mouth, but approached it a little from the side, and just as I was about to grasp its closed jaws the stick I was pressing them together with broke, and before I could jerk my right hand away, the alligator with a snap as quick as a flash, caught the first finger of my hand in its mouth driving two teeth through at the joint. I was lucky enough, as it loosed my finger and made a grab for my hand, to jerk clear; for if it had caught my hand I would probably have lost the use of it.

The digestive juices of an alligator must be very strong for any food swallowed is digested thoroughly. Even bones, hair, feathers and scales are so completely changed in the process of digestion that no trace of them is seen in the excrement. In opening the stomachs of alligators to examine their contents, when the stomach juices have gotten on my hand, I have experienced a severe burning sensation, that persisted for quite an hour or more, and made my skin feel as if rubbed with strong red pepper. Anything swallowed is passed out through the intestines, and nothing is rejected through the mouth, as is the case with some other reptiles.

Some writers claim to have found in alligators' stomachs round pieces of wood or other foreign substances. I think their observations were not complete, for a closer examination of the substances would probably have proven them to be reminant of food that had remained in the stomach after hibernation had begun, and during the several months of inactivity had been molded by the muscular actions of the stomach into a solid mass, dark brown in color and in texture much resembling wood. I have found such objects from the size of a walnut to ones larger than my fist in the stomach of every alligator taken from its den whose stomach was examined during the months of February and March. This mass is gotten rid of later in the year, for I have never seen it present in summer-killed alligators. Small pieces of wood and other foreign substances are frequently swallowed by alligators, for in catching their food, especially if the food is small, the alligator's big jaws scoop up objects of considerable size together with the food, and if the object taken into its mouth is not too large, it is swallowed with the food. As an alligator does not regurgitate, any object swallowed remains in its stomach until dissolved by the strong gastric juices.

It has been stated by a number of writers that there is usually plenty of game fish, and, therefore, good fishing where alligators abound, but I have never seen the reason given for this fact. I have also noted this fact, and I have noted very carefully the reason for it; which is that alligators feed largely on garfish who are sluggish, extremely predatory fish, and protected by nature with such heavy armor that they are not subject to attack by anything in the water except alligators. Alligators certainly destroy great numbers of garfish, and where alligators are plentiful, garfish are scarce, and where garfish are scarce, then game fish such as bass and perch accumulate in numbers.

After hatching, the young take no food for a number of days, and then feed very sparingly on such little fish, insects and other small creatures as they can catch and swallow while in the limited area in which their mother keeps them. I have seen mother alligators catch large fish, large snakes, and turtles in their jaws and crush them to a pulp, holding them at the surface of the water between their jaws, so that the young could gather bits of food from the crushed flesh. The young would grasp the food in their mouths and with vigorous shakes of the head tear off bits of it which they would swallow exactly as the old ones do, by raising their head in the air and gulping down the food. I find in going through my notes on the alligator that I have witnessed this method of young alligators getting food on eight different occasions—four times on garfish, twice on snakes, and twice on turtles.

In catching their food, small alligators lie in wait and with a swift side motion of the head catch insects, crawfish, crabs, fish and other small creatures that may come to them. They also swim after and catch birds and small animals they may see swimming.

Large alligators, that is ones eight feet and more in length, usually hunt their prey. I have seen them, however, lie in wait for fish. In doing this they always place their head counter to the way the tide is running, and on the edge of an exposed flat or sandbar. In this position they wait until a school of fish following the tide close to the bank comes between their tail and the bank, when with a quick sweep of the tail some of the fish may be thrown onto the bank. If a lucky stroke has been made, the alligator then crawls out and picks up his catch with his mouth, throwing up and back his head, swallowing whatever he has captured. In making grabs at the wriggling victim at times the alligator also catches up pieces of driftwood or

ALLIGATORS WHEN HUNTING FOOD SWIM SLOWLY THROUGH THE WATER
WITH ONLY THE TOP OF THE HEAD AND BACK SHOWING.

other substances, and if these are not too large, pays no attention to them, but swallows them together with its prey.

Alligators are death on hogs, and during the days before they had been hunted to an appreciable extent, it was impossible to raise hogs with any success in the districts where alligators were plentiful. At one time I placed a large number of hogs on a ridge in one of our overflow marshes, building for them a considerable pen in which a small amount of feed was spread once a day in order to get the hogs used to seeing people and used to coming to a central point for food. This pen was about one hundred feet from the nearest stream and under a group of large live-oak trees. On three different occasions the man who fed the hogs reported that he saw evidences of alligators having been in the pen during the previous night, and of having captured one or more hogs. The evidence of a considerable battle and the marks of the alligator's body and feet together with blood were signs enough to tell what had happened. The outcome of this experiment of raising hogs in the marsh was that the alligators got so many of them, it was not profitable, so was abandoned.

During the Winter alligators take no food, being dormant, so no damage is done to migratory wild fowl. During the Summer, however, they will catch any bird or animal that they can reach. I have had Canada Geese, Blue Geese and White-fronted Geese as well as Syrus Cranes and African Crown Cranes caught and killed by alligators, and sometimes the alligators who did the killing were not more than four feet long, and the birds they destroyed were far too large for them to swallow.

In feeding, alligators make no attempt to kill their prey with their tails as one would infer from reading the records of those who have written about the alligator. They use their powerful tails only when their intended prey is in such a position that it cannot be readily grasped with its

jaws.   It then strikes at its intended victim with its tail.
As the tail sweeps in an arch towards the head, the head is
thrown in the same direction.   Thus, if the victim is struck
with the tail, it will be swept into grabbing distance of
the jaws.

CHAPTER IV

RATE OF GROWTH AND SIZE

Young alligators are hatched from an egg having a dimension of about two and six-tenths inches long by one and six-tenths inches wide, the average length of the newly-hatched little ones is about nine inches.

Under favorable conditions they grow much more rapidly than naturalists have generally supposed.

The only record I have been able to find of the growth of alligators where the age of the individuals under observation was positively known, was made by Mr. Raymond L. Ditmars, curator of reptiles of the Bronx Zoological Park. In his "Reptile Book," page eighty-six, he gives the average growth and weight of five alligators each year for five years. At the end of the fifth year he states: "The specimens showed an average length of five feet, six inches and weighed fifty pounds." He further states that the alligators were "kept in a large tank heated to a temperature of about 90° F." He further states: "In a wild state growth is undoubtedly more rapid than here noted."

I have, during my study of the alligator, kept accurate records of the rate of growth, both length and weight, of a number of alligators taken from the nest which were weighed, measured, toe-marked for identification and liberated with the mother in a large wooded pond on Avery Island. The following data on their growth is illuminating.

First, we will compare the rate in growth of alligators under natural conditions at Avery Island where they take no food for the five months during hibernation, with those kept in confinement in a regular temperature of about ninety degrees Fahrenheit all the year and fed continuously as described by Ditmars in "The Reptile Book," pages eighty-five and eighty-six.

Two Years Old	Two Years Old
New York, N. Y.	Avery Island, Louisiana
Average length—23 inches Average weight—3 pounds	Average length—40.7 inches Average weight—10 pounds 13 ounces
Five Years Old	
Average length—66 inches Average weight—50 pounds	Four Years Old
Not Given	Average length—62 inches Average weight—24 pounds 15 ounces
	Six Years Old
	Average length—72 inches Average weight—52 pounds

This comparison tends to show that little alligators under natural conditions make a much more rapid growth during the first two years than those in confinement. After the second year those in confinement grow more rapidly and put on more weight than those under natural conditions. Probably because those in confinement are kept in an even temperature and fed through the entire twelve months, and those under natural conditions are dormant and do not feed for the five cold months of each year.

The following comparison is the first record of the difference in the rate of growth in alligators between the sexes. This lot of alligators were toe-marked, measured, weighed and liberated when first hatched, August, 1921. Many of them were caught each year thereafter and their weight and growth recorded up to the sixth year. At the beginning of the sixth year I found they were doing so much

THESE NEWLY HATCHED LITTLE FELLOWS AVERAGE EIGHT AND ONE HALF INCHES IN LENGTH.

damage to the birds and other wild life in my thirty-five acre wild life sanctuary in which they lived, that I thought it advisable to have some of them killed. In August, 1927, I had lines set, on which were tied heavy hooks baited with raw meat and hung about twelve inches above the water. Eleven alligators were taken, killed, weighed, measured, and their stomachs examined, and toe-marks checked during 1927; and others were caught and killed in succeeding years. The average weight and length is below recorded:

Aug. 16, 1927, at 6 yrs. old, 4 males, 6 ft., 5½ in., 68 lbs.
Aug. 16, 1927, at 6 yrs. old, 6 females, 5 ft., 6¾ in., 36 lbs.
Aug. 20, 1930, at 9 yrs. old, 4 males, 8 ft., 3 in., 134 lbs.
Aug. 20, 1930, at 9 yrs. old, 2 females, 6 ft., 8 in., 87 lbs.
July 29, 1931, at 10 yrs. old, 3 males, 9 ft., 2 in., 251 lbs.
July 29, 1931, at 10 yrs. old, 2 females, 7 ft., 3 in., 113 lbs.

This comparison points to the conclusion that male alligators at least from the sixth year on, grow both in length and weight much more rapidly than the females.

On July 15, 1932, when eleven years old, one of this lot of alligators, a male, was killed that measured ten feet, one inch, and weighed 354 pounds.

There is plenty of evidence in the written records of long past observers that alligators in Louisiana attain an extreme length of, at least, eighteen or twenty feet. To my certain knowledge, there has been taken in the vicinity of Avery Island, three alligators exceeding eighteen feet in length. One of these was an alligator known to we boys as "Monsurat," killed by Mr. Robert Moony at Avery Island in 1879, which was measured by my father. This alligator was eighteen feet, three inches in length. The next large one that I remember seeing measured, was killed by Robert Dell, our plantation overseer, in October, 1882, at the junction of the road across the marsh joining Avery Island with the mainland, at the Avery Island end. Dell was coming in over the road and saw this alligator crossing the road.

He had a pistol with him, and shot the alligator from his horse, killing it. On his describing its size to my father and uncles, a four-mule team and wagon was sent to bring it to our house. This alligator measured eighteen feet, five and one-half inches. The third large alligator which I know to have been above eighteen feet was killed by me on January 2, 1890, in a small bayou which had connected Lake Cock with Vermilion Bay. The mouth of this bayou where it had joined the bay had become closed by the '79 storm, and at the time I killed this alligator, there was no opening from the bayou into the bay, as the beach ridge had formed across the mouth, and grass had grown in the bayou for perhaps three hundred feet back of the beach. I had started on a goose hunt in a lugger with two assistants; being overtaken at dusk without sufficient breeze to go further, we anchored just off the place where Bayou Cock had emptied into Vermilion Bay. As this was a famous duck country, and as the water was shallow, I waded ashore to get some ducks for supper. Walking back into the marsh along the border of the old bayou, I killed a couple of mallards which fell in the grass that had grown up in the bayou. On wading in to retrieve them, I saw in front of me what I thought, in the dim light after sundown, was a partly submerged log. On going up to it, I found it was an enormous alligator almost completely dormant in the cold air and water. I shot it directly through the head and on lifting its head from the muddy water, was convinced that it was the largest alligator I had ever seen. The next morning with my two companions and some rope, we went back to the place where I had killed the alligator, tied the rope around its neck and tried to pull it through the very boggy marsh to the solid bank to skin it, but the three of us, owing to its great size and weight, could not do more than move it a short distance, as when we would exert ourselves to pull on the rope, we would bog down in the soft mud past our knees. I finally gave up trying to get the alligator out, but it was so large that I took the barrel off my gun and measured it with the gun barrel which was thirty inches in length, marking with my knife by a cut on the back every point where the end of the gun barrel stopped. After measuring the alligator three times in order to prove the previous measures, I found the length to be nineteen feet, two inches. This is the largest alligator I have ever known of being actually measured. This alligator must have been very old and had probably left his den in the Summer and was unable to get back to it, and would probably have died from exposure that Winter. His teeth were worn down almost to the jaw bone, and the stumps very badly discolored. Another large alligator caught at Avery Island measuring seventeen feet, three inches was brought to my uncle, John Avery, alive in 1886. My uncle built a crate for this alligator and sent it North by boat, alive, directed to the Smithsonian Institution, as the authorities of that institution had requested some member of my family to secure for them a very large alligator. This alligator was put on deck of one of the Morgan line steamers going to Philadelphia. During the trip up, there was considerable painting being done on the ship, and one of the sailors poured part of a can of green paint over the alligator's back, rubbing it in with his brush. The alligator died and was thrown overboard before reaching its destination.

The last very large alligator I have record of was killed on Marsh Island, by Max Touchet in March, 1916. Max who had been supervising game-warden for Marsh Island for several years, told me of having found the den of an alligator a considerable distance back in the marsh between Bayou Chin and Bayou Mechow. He had seen this alligator a number of times as it basked in the sun on the bank near its den, and thought it was at least eighteen feet in length. I told him to catch the alligator and if it was seventeen feet long I would give him two hundred dollars for it, alive and in good condition. At the end of the trap-

ping season in the Spring of 1916, Max and another man
with a pole and hook pulled this alligator out of his den,
and tied him up; but he was so heavy they could not pull him
to the nearest bayou which was about three miles away; so
they killed him and brought me the skin. The skin, without stretching, measured seventeen feet, ten inches with
about four inches off the end of the tail and the bone of the
nose extended at least four inches beyond the point where
the skin began on the under jaw. I had this skin tanned
which caused it to shrink somewhat, but it still measures
seventeen feet, nine inches as is shown in the photograph
accompanying this article.

I am sure these large alligators just referred to were of
exceptional size and much larger than normal, and were
very old individuals, probably older and larger than alligators will ever again attain. I think about fifteen feet in
length is the normal size male alligators should reach,
as there were many of about this size in the early
days before they were destroyed by hide-hunters; but
to attain a size of fifteen feet an alligator must, I
think, live for at least thirty to forty years, as we know
the rate of growth in the males under normal conditions is
about one foot a year up to a length of nine or ten feet, and
after this length is reached the average growth per year
is not more than a very few inches. Because of the extensive
hunting of these creatures for their skins, and the ease, due
to internal combustion engines, with which skin-hunters can
reach the most distant and secluded sections, it is extremely
doubtful if an alligator will be allowed to live long enough
to attain maximum size.

I have for many years kept a number of large alligators
in confinement in as near a natural condition as possible,
and have tried in every way to get alive very large individuals. I have a standing offer of one hundred dollars
for every thirteen foot alligator brought to me in good condition, and an offer of a bonus of fifty dollars a foot for each

THE ALLIGATOR FROM WHICH THIS SKIN WAS TAKEN MEASURED MORE THAN EIGHTEEN FEET. KILLED ON MARSH ISLAND, 1916, BY MAX TOUCHET.

foot in length above thirteen feet. This offer is known to all regular alligator hunters of Louisiana and Texas and has been standing for more than twenty years. During that time one thirteen footer has been brought me, plenty of eleven and twelve footers, but none larger. There has hardly been a Summer since I first made this offer that I have not received word of the capture of fourteen foot, fifteen foot and larger alligators, but on sending to measure them, they have been found to be from ten and one-half to twelve feet in length. It is amazing how the length of an alligator shrinks when a tape line is stretched along his back!

The weight of a male alligator is not always in proportion to his length, for one type grows long and slender and another has less length and more thickness. So there may be great differences in the weight of alligators having the same length. Then again the time for weighing has much to do with the weight for length. A ten foot alligator weighed in April shortly after he had come out of winter quarters will always weigh much less than the same alligator if he had been weighed in the Fall when full of fat and prepared to go into his den for the Winter. As he eats nothing for five months, it is only natural that considerable weight is lost during the hibernating period.

The measurements and weights of three large male alligators I now have, were as follows on July 15, 1932:

Grandpa, 11 ft., 6 inches—weighed 591 lbs.
Jim, 11 ft., 9½ inches—weighed 486½ lbs.
Big-Boy, 12 ft., 1 inch—weighed 460 lbs.

Grandpa is much the oldest of the three and is one of the short heavy type. Big-Boy is the youngest of the three and is one of the long slender type. I think Big-Boy will exceed fifteen feet in length at thirty years, he is now about sixteen years old.

The adult female alligator is much smaller than the male. The largest female I have ever seen measured nine feet, one and one-half inches, and weighed 163½ pounds. I have never heard of one larger. The next largest was eight feet, ten inches, and I have measured many that were a full eight feet and one or two inches. In late years I have caught, measured and liberated many female alligators at their nests to try to determine how small they are when they begin laying. The smallest I have ever found nesting was six feet, three inches, which would mean a seven year old.

During the past eight years I have caused to be examined more than one hundred and seventy-five female alligators killed on my property during the breeding season, and the smallest found with eggs was six feet, one inch. This leads me to believe that female alligators do not breed until they are six years old, and possibly seven years old.

It is a fact well known to all old alligator hunters that the length of an alligator can be very accurately told if one is a good judge of measure and can see the alligators head; for the distance from the forward edge of its eye to its nose in inches is about the length of the alligator in feet.

The alligator's head shown opposite page 64, is from one that measured fourteen feet, eleven inches, while the ruler resting on it shows the head to be fifteen inches from eye to end of nose.

The alligator's head shown opposite page 65, is from one that measured thirteen feet, eight inches, and the rule resting on it shows fourteen inches.

This alligator was pulled from its den with a pole and killed with two blows of a hand axe by Emar Broussard, in the cypress swamp east of Avery Island in September, 1925. One cut of the axe can be seen across both jaws well back, and a cut just below and back of the left eye which was fatal. A section of bone was split from the alligator's head by the last blow and can be seen in the photograph still attached

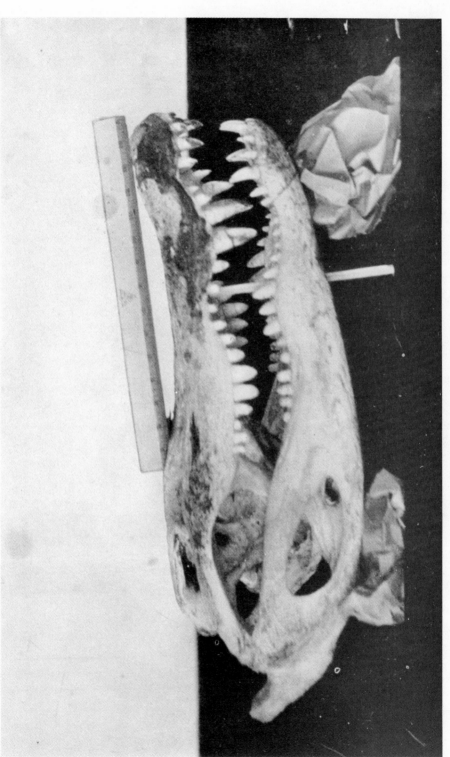

THE SKULL OF AN ALLIGATOR THAT MEASURED FOURTEEN FEET, ELEVEN INCHES.

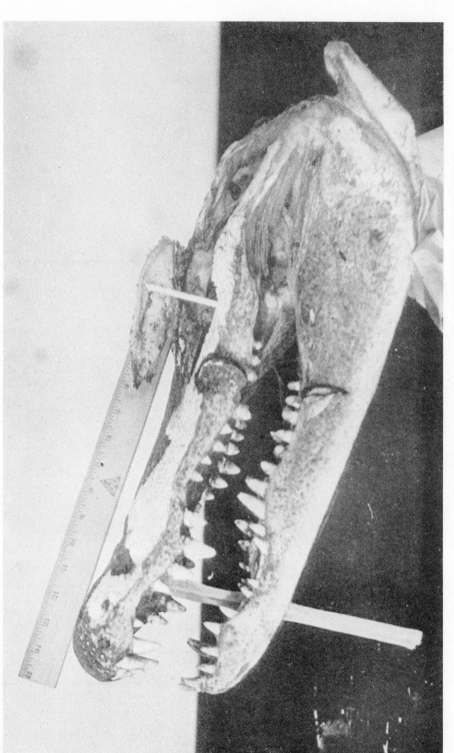

THE SKULL OF A THIRTEEN FOOT, EIGHT INCH ALLIGATOR PULLED FROM ITS DEN AND KILLED WITH A HAND AXE.

to the skull by the upper skin and held up by the small white stick.

It is very rare that alligator hunters bring to market the skin of a really long alligator. The hunter is paid no more for a twelve foot skin than for a seven foot skin, and is paid very little more for a seven foot skin than for a six foot or a five foot skin. It is generally the practice of the alligator hunter, in order to get the most from a large skin, to cut it diagonally in two, then each part will be graded by its actual length. In other words—If a hunter kills a twelve foot alligator he cuts the skin so as to get two seven foot pieces from the one by cutting the skin in a diagonal manner from a point forward of the front leg to such a point on the tail that it will net him two seven foot pieces, and the buyer pays full price for two seven foot skins. For this reason, very few large whole alligator skins go to market. During 1933 a hunter on Marsh Island killed a fifteen foot alligator, the skin of which he cut in such a manner that he got two seven foot and one six foot pieces of hide.

CHAPTER V

TEETH

Alligators are provided with large, strong teeth, deeply set in both lower and upper jaw. There are thirty-eight to forty in the upper jaw and the same number in the lower jaw. The forward teeth in both jaws are pointed and set in individual sockets, these are used for catching and holding their food. The rear teeth in both jaws are blunt and conical, set in grooves in the jaws, and are used for crushing food that cannot be swallowed whole. Several teeth of the lower jaw back of the ninth tooth on each side are slanted backward to facilitate getting bulky food in proper position for being swallowed. The teeth are without roots, and in immature individuals the tips only are shed. As the reptile grows, that portion of the teeth which is inside the bone part of the jaw is absorbed. The caps of the new teeth forming inside and under each other and grow up inside the old teeth to take place of the old teeth as they become obsolete.

In the photograph of the teeth, opposite page 66, all taken from a fifteen foot alligator, reading from left to right:

No. 1, is the left ninth from front upper tooth fully growing, showing in the arched opening in its base the tips of a new tooth developing.

No. 2, is the right ninth from front upper tooth, showing by its frayed lower edges and its rough outside that it has begun to be absorbed to give place to.

No. 3, the new right ninth from front upper tooth already one-third developed growing from under and inside it.

No. 6, is the tenth tooth from upper right jaw fully developed, with tip of new tooth showing inside and in arched opening at base.

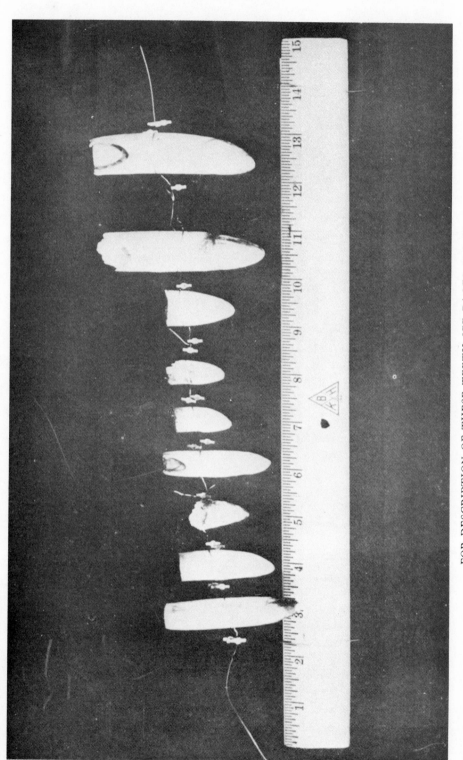

FOR DESCRIPTION OF THESE TEETH SEE PAGES 66 & 67.

No. 4, is the top of upper left tenth tooth the base of which has almost been absorbed. Only a very small part of this tooth was still in the jaw socket, the rest having been absorbed, and the tip held in place by the gum would have soon been pushed out by the new tooth growing up.

No. 5, is the new upper left tenth tooth which was in place under number four.

No. 7, is tip or cap of upper front fourth tooth whose below the gum surface has been almost completely absorbed, the tip shown being held in place only by the gum.

No. 8, is new upper left front fourth tooth about one-half developed which was growing under top or cap number seven, and almost ready to take its place.

No. 9, is the upper right fourth tooth fully developed, and showing a small thin egg-shaped space near its inside base at which point absorbation of the tooth's bony structure begins as the new tooth develops inside, the tiny cap of a new tooth is in place inside this tooth.

There are often tips of three new teeth under each other and inside the hollow base of the old tooth. As the jaw grows and the old teeth become too small for their sockets the hollow bases up to the exposed solid points are absorbed and disintegrated while still in place and the new teeth growing up have nothing to *push out,* but push off the solid caps which are the only part of the old teeth really shed.

When an alligator becomes fully grown, its teeth give evidence of maturity by becoming almost solid; that is, in growing alligators, the teeth are hollow and changed often. In fully-grown specimens the teeth are no longer changed, and are solid almost all the way down. This is the only way I know of by which a fully-grown alligator can be distinguished from one not yet mature.

All the teeth of the upper jaw overlap the teeth of the lower jaw, and when the jaws are closed the teeth of the lower jaw are completely hidden by those of the upper jaw.

The fourth tooth from the front on each side of the

lower jaw is much longer than any other tooth of the lower set, and fits into a depression of the upper jaw. Occasionally in very large alligators this fourth tooth is of such length that it punctures the upper jaw and its tip is in evidence above the upper jaw. In the upper jaw the ninth tooth on each side from the front is much the largest and longest of the entire set. The next largest of the entire set being the eighth tooth on each side of the upper set.

CHAPTER VI

VOICE

The vocal ability of the alligator is exceedingly limited. Their vocal chords are a pair of membranous folds inside the glottis, which allows them to make only three sounds audible to the human ear—the "umph, umph, umph," a call used from the day of hatching through maturity; the quavering, sighing hiss given when angry; and the bellow of the bulls which seem to be more a challenge to rivals than for any other purpose, and may be long drawn out, lasting seconds, or only a short deep cough.

At the time the little alligators are ready to come out of the egg, but before they are actually hatched, they make an audible grunting sound—umph, umph, umph, which sound can be imitated exactly by the human voice if this syllable is pronounced in a high key, with the lips closed. This grunting sound is a signal to the mother that the little ones are about ready to emerge from the egg, and the mother with her jaws removes six to ten inches of the nest-material from over the eggs so that the little ones, as they hatch, can have easy access to the open world.

That the mature alligators use the same shrill grunting "umph" as is used in youth was brought to my notice as follows:

In May, 1892, I witnessed the last part of a fight between two large bulls, both of which I captured alive. One of them measured nine feet, eight inches, and was very heavy of body with an unusually large head; the other measured eleven feet, five inches, and was much more slender. By the conformation and size of the head, I think the shorter one was the older of the two. I was attracted to this fight while paddling a pirogue along a bayou near home, by hearing a great rustling and thrashing about in the marsh grass. Leaving my boat and following the sound, I came to two alligators fighting in the high marsh grass, perhaps one hundred feet back from the bayou. They must have been fighting for some time as a good lot of the grass was mashed down over a space about forty feet square. When I got to them the fight was almost over, for the smaller one had caught the larger one across the body just back of the front legs and had driven his large teeth completely through the heavy bony plates which cover all alligators' backs, and was slowly but surely squeezing the life out of his larger antagonist, who could not reach his opponent with either head or tail. The large alligator was crying in a shrill voice, "umph-umph-umph," exactly as if he was saying: "Enough!" I went back to my pirogue, got an iron-shod pole that I always kept in the boat and some rope, tied the jaws of the big fellow first, and with the pole beat the other over the head until he loosed his hold, then quickly tied his jaws together, and driving the pole deeply into the ground, tied both of them to it. The small alligator showed a very great desire to again attack the larger one, and the larger one tried to run away. Having securely fastened them, I went for help and a larger boat, and soon had them safely penned.

The roar or bellow of the male alligator is a challenge to others of his species, and is not given for the purpose of attracting the opposite sex. The mating season extends from early April into June, and the alligator roars more frequently during that period and less often throughout the Summer, and they also occasionally roar on warm mornings or very warm nights during the Winter. Their roar is seldom heard, however, in December, January and February, although I have heard it during these months.

During the mating season when the male roars the female often gives a rattling sound exactly like a man snoring, only a bit louder, and sounding like the word "snar-r-r" if pronounced in a deep voice. I have never heard a female alligator roar or bellow. The male seems to be the only one who uses this method of expression.

The deep booming roar of a twelve foot male alligator is a sound that once heard will never be forgotten. It is not unlike the first boom note of the ostrich, or the deep, slow-throat roar of the lion before he begins the quick short-cough roars; but exceeds in volume both of these sounds. It has much more volume and is deeper in tone than the bellow of the largest of our domestic bulls. I know of no sound, natural or artificial, that causes such a tremendous vibration of the atmosphere as the full-throated roar of a full-grown alligator. Often when near these reptiles as they bellowed, I have felt a very distinct vibration of my diaphragm caused by the trembling of the air by the broken waves of sound thrown out by these great creatures.

I have very many times witnessed big male alligators roaring, and this sound is given generally when the beast is in the water; but sometimes also when his head and part of his body is on the bank. I have never heard one roar when entirely out of the water, and have seen big, old bulls slip off the bank into the water and roar in answer to the roar of some other alligator calling near by. The preliminary movement is a quick upward surge of the entire body as it is filled with air taken in through the nostrils. When thoroughly inflated, a large portion of the body about one-third of the thickness from nose to tail rises above the surface of the water. The second movement is a throwing up of the head so that it is entirely above the water at a sharp angle to the body, and with probably half the neck elevated at an angle of about twenty-five degrees. The tail is also elevated above the water at the same time, with sometimes the tip arching down to the water and a considerable portion of its length is waved from side to side while in the air. The side skin of an alligator is made up of

tough horny plates, not overlapping, but lying side by side
and joined together by a soft connecting skin. Over the
back and neck the covering is hard plates of bone (ridged
down the centre) lying in parallel rows and set in the soft
body skin. As the great reptile throws itself into the position of roaring—body tightly inflated, throat puffed to its
fullest extent, head and tail up; the central part of the body
sinks below the water with the uplifting of the head and tail,
and its entire body cavity is contracted with a series of
powerful spasmodic jerks. This contraction forces the air
with which its body is distended through the throat and out
the mouth which is open only from an inch to an inch and
one-half, and rapidly vibrates the membranous folds inside
the glottis causing a tremendous volume of sound. The
time it takes to give this roar covers perhaps three and
one-half to seven seconds; beginning as a moderate tone and
increasing until the full volume of sound is reached and then
decreasing to the end. When this great sound is given, if
the alligator's body is entirely in the water, a phenomenon
occurs which is the most curious thing of its kind I have ever
witnessed. When the alligator throws its head and tail
above the surface of the water preparatory to giving its
roar, the central part of its body which had been above the
surface of the water, because of its having been greatly
distended with air, sinks below the surface, and the violent
muscular contraction of the body which forces the air out
of its mouth causing the roar, and which contraction is made
in spasmodic jerks, contracts the flexible skin of its sides so
violently that the water lying against this skin and between
the horny scales of the sides and edge of the back is driven
in jets above the surface for a couple of inches, in drops the
size of the end of one's little finger, giving exactly the im-
pression one gets when looking at a surface of smooth water
on which large drops of heavy rain are falling—the drops
are seen bouncing into the air from the water. Small waves
also radiate in all directions as if heavy objects were being

thrown into the water. This leaping and shimmering of the water above the alligator's back as the bellow is given is something that when once seen can never be forgotten, and may be duplicated by a person in a small way, if the hand is placed a couple of inches under water half open, palm up and then closed violently.

The bellowing of a big alligator may be continued at intervals of a couple of minutes until a dozen or more calls have been made, and if there are other large male 'gators in hearing, it is very certain they will raise their voices in answer. When a number of large bulls are roaring at the same time the volume of sound is truly great. During still nights I have heard alligators roaring at least three miles distant.

In early May, 1895, I was out with a party of alligator hunters who had located a nesting of Roseate Spoonbills for me, near Lake Misere in Cameron Parish, Louisiana. We were camped at the point where Bayou Misere and the lake come together, and had killed a number of alligators that night with the aid of headlights. Just at daylight we heard a chorus of deep alligator voices in the lake not far from us, and each time they roared they seemed to be nearer. As soon as it was light enough, we saw a line of alligators, all big ones, a couple of hundred yards out in the lake, headed for the bayou. Suddenly, the second in line from the front threw his head and tail in the air and roared, seven others that were in line behind him did the same thing, each roaring three times. They were following about fifty feet behind each other. Once more they all roared when the leader was only about fifty yards from our camp. I got out my rifle prepared to do some shooting as they passed into the bayou, which would bring them in about twenty yards from where we sat. The owner of the boat who was an old-time alligator hunter asked me not to shoot the leader, as it was a female, and said that if I shot her the others would go back. He said he had often seen a number of male alligators following a female, and if he did not kill the female he could be sure of getting all the males, and that on two occasions when he killed the female first, the following males went under the water, and he got none of them. Therefore, I let the female pass and killed the eight males as they swam pass camp. All of these males were more than eight feet long, and the one next to the female measured twelve feet, eleven inches.

The big bulls also make, when looking for a fight, a peculiar half-roar half-hiss. This noise is given with a sudden inflation of the body and a quick surge forward accompanied by two tremendous whacks of the tail right and left, and at the same time (without raising the head completely out of the water, as when roaring) giving voice to a deep, short, throaty cough followed by a deep reverberating "er-r-r-r." This noise is not often heard, and I think is a challenge to possible rivals, for after making the sound, which is never repeated immediately, as is the roar, the one giving it holds his head high above and parallel to the water with a fierce expectant look, as if looking for trouble.

All alligators, both male and female, when danger approaches or when getting ready to fight with others, inflate themselves and then blow the air through the nostrils, making a loud hissing sound. This sound is only for the purpose of challenging an opponent or to frighten away something that they consider dangerous. This is the only sound I have ever heard given by the female, except the "umph," which they use in different tones when calling their young, and the "sna-r-r-r" in answer to the roar of the male in the breeding season. This "umph" sound by its tones seem to have various meanings, as I have heard it used by female alligators to assemble their young and to warn them also. It is also the sound given by the young when badly frightened, and will cause the mother alligator to come to the rescue of the little ones. This sound is the only one used by an alligator when in pain from wounds.

When a bull alligator roars, it, on raising its head above the water, opens the two musk glands located in the skin under and on each side near the bones of the lower jaw, and throws off a considerable quantity of sweet pungent-smelling musk that not only scents the air but the surface of the water as well, and lingers as a strong perfume in the vicinity for some hours. There is positively nothing visable in the throwing off of this musk, such as has been described in many of the written records of alligators. The female does not seem to make use of the jaw musk glands of the under neck, except when fighting to protect her nest or young or herself, but does throw off, during the mating season, a considerable amount of strong sweet-smelling musk from two musk glands located in the inside wall on each side of the cloaca. The musk glands of both the lower jaw and the cloaca are filled with a thick brownish-yellow waxy mass that is exposed to the air at will by the individual, by the spreading of the opening of the glands and a contraction of the muscles surrounding them. At such a time the inside of the glands are forced out so that they appear as a rough brown mass above the surface of the body skin, and at this time the air is filled with the musky odor, by coming in contact with the exposed musk surface; there is no spraying of musk as a jet into the air.

CHAPTER VII

Enemies

After alligators reach a length of three or four feet they have no enemies, with the exception of man. Before the eggs are hatched, the nests are subject to attack and the eggs to be eaten by a number of animals. 'Coons, opossums, skunks, hogs and bears are all fond of alligator eggs, and if the mother is killed before her eggs hatch, there is very little change for the young to develop, as the nest is almost certain to be opened by some of the various animals who eat eggs, and if the nest is opened and the eggs exposed to the air the embryos will die, even if the eggs themselves are not all eaten. After the young alligators are hatched, they may be preyed upon by garfish or other large fish, and to a certain extent they may be preyed upon by individuals of their own kind. The young alligators are also eaten by 'coons, as I have a number of times seen 'coons catch young alligators under fourteen inches in length that were on the edge of the banks, and with a swift crunch of the jaw bite through the skull. The only thing eaten by the 'coon is the minute brain.

Man has caused the almost extermination of the alligator in large sections of Louisiana, where once they fairly swarmed. In the late Seventies and early Eighties, before there had been any hunting of alligators on the many thousands of acres belonging to my family surrounding Avery Island, they were present in unbelievable numbers; and the children of the place grew up in intimate association with them, as we saw them every day and swam in the same waters with them, had special names for many of them, and when swimming in the bayou below the house, always brought them to us by imitating the grunting call, which is the only sound made universally by alligators, or by imitating the bark or cry of a dog.

The first alligator hunters came to the vicinity of Avery Island in 1883. At that time only skins of eight feet or larger were taken, and the universal price was one dollar per skin for anything from eight feet up. The method of hunting them was for two hunters to go out during dark nights in a small flat-bottomed boat; one man sitting in the front facing forward, armed with a double barrel shotgun loaded with number four shot, and wearing on his hat, what was then known as a bull's eye lamp, burning lard oil, and a man in the back who propelled the boat. In this manner they proceeded along the bayous after dark. The light from the bull's-eye would be reflected by the eyes of an alligator which showed as red or yellow spots on the dark water. The man in the rear would generally not see the eyes, but the man in front would motion with his hand the direction that the boat was to be propelled. The alligator being blinded by the light could not see the boat, and a very near approach could be made. When the boat was near enough, usually not more than six or eight feet from the alligator, the top of its head would be blown off with the concentrated load from the shotgun. The man who did the shooting would at once put down his gun, take up a short heavy pole to which was attached, on each side of one end, a sharpened hook made of one-fourth inch iron, which he would put under the alligator and draw it to the boat, or if the alligator had sunk, he would feel along the bottom with the pole until it was located, get one of the hooks under the body, and with a quick jerk drive it into the skin, pulling the alligator to the surface. When an alligator is shot through the brain, it does not sink immediately but turns belly up with its two front feet stuck straight up in the air. It will stay in this position for several minutes, then gradually settle out of sight under the water. Having drawn the alligator to the side of the boat, the man in the bow would catch it by the nose and if it was not too large—that is, not more than nine or ten feet long—would slide it over the side into the boat. As soon as the alligator was gotten into the boat, a cut was made across the back immediately behind the hind legs and through the vertebrae with a sharp hand axe or hatchet. This cut was made in order to keep the alligator from thrashing about, as they often do for some time after being shot through the brain; for a large alligator in its dying struggles is not a very safe companion in a small boat. If the alligator was too large to take into the boat, it was pulled on the bank, a small rope tied to a front leg, and to the grass or bushes on the bank, and it was left to be retrieved in the morning. After the boat was loaded, it was propelled by paddle or oars back to the hunters' camp which might be on the bank of the stream or in a larger boat.

In the morning the alligators were skinned by making a cut from the underside of the chin along both sides of the lower jaw, then around the head below the eyes to the heavy bony plates of the neck, then down each side following the edge of the bone plates of the back to where these plates end a short distance back of the hind legs. The cut then extended along the upper edge of the tail to its end. The cut having been completed, if the alligator was a large one, the two men immediately started the work of skinning, and as they always kept a whetstone suspended from their belts with which they kept the skinning knives sharp, this work progressed very rapidly. When the skin was taken off, it was at once thickly covered with salt on the flesh side, and then rolled up, beginning from the head to the tail, the sides being turned in as the rolling proceeded. These skins were then packed in the hole of the boat or in a special part of the camp. When a sufficient number had been taken they were disposed of at one of the towns on the larger streams making from the Gulf to interior Louisiana. The principal towns in which the alligator skins were sold, beginning at the western part of the State, were Lake Charles, Abbeville, New Iberia, Morgan City, Houma and New Orleans. It would be interesting to know how many alligator skins were marketed from these towns from the period between 1880 and 1933. I fully believe the number would reach at least three to three and one-half million.

The carcasses of the alligators were, of course, made no use of, but were thrown into the stream where they floated until eventually they either decomposed or were eaten by crabs or buzzards. Some few hunters piled the heads on the bank and went back later in the year to gather up the teeth, which had a small market value.

Up to about 1898, this was the only method used in taking alligators in Louisiana. About 1898 the large alligators inhabiting the streams became scarce, and as the price for the skins was good, the hunters began going into the marshes for them and getting them out of their lairs or dens. It must be understood that a great many alligators do not come to the streams at any time during their lives, but stay in small ponds or landlocked lakes in the swamps and marshes. These alligators were captured by an entirely different method.

The first thing the marsh hunter does, is to set fire to the grass and burn off a large area of the wet prairie. These men usually hunt in pairs. They proceed over the marsh, each man armed with a fifteen to eighteen foot pole made of a straight cypress or Tupelo gum sapling, and very occasionally with a pole worked down from a piece of cut timber. The length of these poles is never less than twelve feet and sometimes is as much as eighteen feet in length. The pole is as near straight as possible, and about two and one-half inches in diameter. One end of the pole has firmly attached to it a hook made of a strong iron rod about one-half inch in diameter, turned so that it will measure about three inches across the curve, and very sharply pointed.

The hunters having located an alligator hole can easily tell by the signs on the bank and the condition of the water whether or not it is occupied, and by the signs they can also tell approximately the size of the occupant.

Having located a hole in which there was an alligator, the hunter proceeded to feel with his pole until he found the opening from the water, that led under the marsh or bank to the alligator's den. He then ran his pole in as far as possible, and if he did not encounter the alligator, noted the direction that the underground den took, and following this line to about where his pole would end, would dig through the surface with a small, short-handled shovel that he carried in his belt, making a small opening through the turf into the water of the underground passageway. He would then start at this point and feel farther back into the den with his pole. Sometimes he would have to make two or three openings before he would locate the alligator at the end of the den, and sometimes the den would have several branches or a second opening connecting with a stream or pond, and the alligator would not be found. If the alligator was located, this could be told by its movement which could be felt as the pole touched it. The pole was moved backward and forward until the alligator became enraged, and grabbed the end of it in its mouth. When this happened, the hunter with a quick tug would fasten the iron hook on the end of the pole in the alligator's throat, and if it was not too large, draw it to the entrance that the pole went into. As soon as the alligator's head came above the water, a quick cut from a hand axe through the brain put an end to its life. It was then hauled out in the grass and skinned at once. In this way the hunters would proceed over a considerable territory and frequently get a dozen or more alligator hides in a day. Sometimes they hook on to a very large, powerful alligator that could not be pulled from its den, and occasionally a hunter would lose his pole, as the alligator would be so strong that he would twist the pole out of the hunter's hand and pull it down into the den.

Occasionally an alligator hunter would become careless; and I have known of men to be severely bitten by small alligators whom they tried to kill by breaking their necks, by putting a foot on their heads and catching hold of the tail, and with a strong pull of the tail dislocate the neck vertebrae. Sometimes an alligator would get its head out from under the hunter's foot and catch hold of his leg or foot and give him a severe bite. Even a five or six foot alligator can inflict a painful wound, as its teeth are many and very sharp, but one of this size has not sufficient weight to be really dangerous.

In the old days no small alligators were taken, but now anything that can be skinned is killed.

Old alligators are now very shy of man, and as they usually have large underground tunnels in which to hide, they sometimes cannot be gotten either by light or by pole, and an alligator who has been shot at once by the light of a bull's-eye is never again approachable with a light. As soon as an alligator that has been shot at but not killed sees a headlight, it sinks under the water. These alligators are known as "blinkers," and are entirely shy of night hunters. They are caught, however, by a different method, which is a baited hook. When a hunter finds an alligator that is a "blinker," or whose hole for some reason or other is such that it cannot be caught with a pole, he kills a bird or catches a fish and baits with it a very heavy strong hook, to which he attaches a one-fourth inch rope eight or ten feet in length. This rope is firmly tied to a tree growing on the bank or to a strong stake driven into the earth. It is then looped up and the bait hung about one foot above the water from a forked limb stuck in the bank. The alligator seeing this bait will swim to it and readily take it. Having taken the bait into its mouth, it throws up its head and swallows bait, hook and all. Of course, as soon as it moves off, the line tightens, and the hook sinks into the flesh of the stomach. Sometimes the alligator will roll and wind the line around its body until it draws itself out on the bank, and its contortions are so powerful that when the line becomes tightly wound around its body up to the stake or tree, if the alligator is a large one, it will sometimes either break the line or what it is fastened to and temporarily get away, but the hook in its insides is always fatal, and an alligator that has swallowed a hook is sure to die, and usually crawls out on the bank to die. I have a number of times seen alligators, thus hooked, crawl out on the bank and die without any appreciable amount of struggling.

In the old days when alligators were very plentiful, a crowd of boys and I would take, what we called a red-fish line, being a cotton line about one-fourth inch in diameter, and tie on the end a strong hook, baiting it with a piece of raw meat or a bird, and tie a bottle or cypress stick immediately at the hook for a float. We would call an alligator to us as near as possible, and often several would come within a few yards of us, when we would throw the baited hook with its float as near as we could to the head of the largest, several boys keeping hold of the other end of the line, which was usually about forty or fifty feet long. The alligator would grab the bait and float, and if the float was a bottle, would crush it with its jaws as if it was paper, and then swallow the remnants of glass and baited hook. We would then tighten the line and a great battle would ensue, which always ended by our drawing the alligator to the bank and killing it with an axe or other heavy implement. We, in those days, thought this was sport, and I am detailing this incident to show how plentiful and unafraid of human beings alligators were in the early Eighties.

Some alligator hunters have absolutely no fear of alligators, claiming that if they are careful they can catch the largest of alligators with their hands. Alpha LeBlanc, who now lives at Avery Island with his large family, has, during the past years, been a famous alligator catcher. He would go into the marsh with his partner, armed with a pole and hook for pulling alligators out of their holes, and, unless the alligator was an unusually large one, Alpha would never condescend to use the pole; that is, providing the alligator was not too far back in its den. He would go in to the hole quietly, feeling with his feet and hands until he located the alligator, and would then slowly slip his hand along the alligator's body until he came to its head, and getting his hand under its head, would feel along until he located the nose, then grasping it by the nose, would pull it to him and out of the hole, with a series of quick jerks. As soon as the alligator was in shallow water on the edge of the bank, he would kill it with his hand axe. Alpha has caught hundreds of alligators in this manner, and has never been bitten.

Alligators rarely attack human beings, and during my long life among them, I have only twice suffered unprovoked attacks by them, and I am not too sure that one of these attacks was not a provoked attack, but I was too young and too frightened to know whether the attacking alligator was a female protecting its nest or whether the attack was made without cause. The incident was:—My cousin, John Avery, and I were paddling a small pirogue through a swampy pond on Avery Island known as Willow Pond, when suddenly an alligator that seemed very large to us, rushed at us from the side, struck the rickety little boat and turned it over. Both of us scrambled off through the shallow water and willow trees as fast as we could, but the alligator showed no desire to follow. This makes me think that it was an old female protecting her nest.

The other attack was, I know, without cause. I had been shooting Jacksnipe in the marshes west of Avery Island and was paddling my pirogue down a deep, very narrow bayou, in the last week of March. I had seen a number of alligators, but paid no attention to them, when in a comparatively straight reach of the bayou I saw a very large alli-

gator slide off the bank about one hundred yards ahead,
look at me for a few moments and then disappear under
the water. I was paddling my boat from the left side and
holding very close to the bank. The alligator had slid off
from that side. Suddenly when I came near the place where
I had seen it disappear, the tail of a very large alligator rose
above the water and struck a glancing blow on the side of
my boat, upsetting the boat and driving me against the bank.
I had my loaded gun in front of me with its stock across
one thigh and its barrel extending along the bottom of the
boat. As the alligator struck the boat, I instinctively
dropped the paddle and grabbed the gun, and as I was
driven against the bank, I came to my feet in water not
more than two or three feet deep, simultaneously with the
rising to the surface of the head and neck of the alligator,
not more than six feet from me. The look in its eyes and
the position of its head—being extended well above the
water and parallel to it—showed that it was looking for me
with the intention of grabbing me. Quick as a flash I whirled
my gun and shot it through the head, killing it. I am firmly
convinced that this alligator made an attempt to catch me.
I pulled it to the side of the bank and found it was a very
large one, perhaps eleven or twelve feet long, with a good
section of its tail missing. Large alligators often have a
considerable part of their tail or a leg missing, it having
been twisted off during a fight with one of its kind.

On another occasion, I had been shooting Upland Plover
in late August, and I was riding back from the prairie over
the road through the marsh connecting Avery Island with
the highland, when I saw an old alligator with a lot of young
ones crossing the road in front of me. I had with me a
young darky who was carrying my game, and riding another
horse. We 'loped up quickly as I wanted to get some of the
young ones, but the whole party slid off the road into the
water bordering the road before I got to them. I jumped
off my horse, handed the reins and my gun to the boy who

was with me, and began looking along the bank hoping to find some of the little ones. Close to the bank I saw four or five of them on the edge of the water against the grass. I lay down very foolishly and began crawling on my stomach, trying to get close enough to grab the little fellows without frightening them. The boy on the horse suddenly called out: "Look out for the big one, Boss." I raised my head just in time to avoid the rush of the mother alligator, who, to protect her young, had risen to the surface and rushed at me, and but for the timely call of the boy, would undoubtedly have got me by the head, and that would have been the last of me, as she was a big one. This instance was clearly an attack in protection of the young.

Alligators have exceedingly acute hearing and sight, and I am sure, can see the approach of a person long before they can be seen by the person. A number of times I have witnessed alligators disappearing off the bank of streams long before I could see them on the bank. As I would be paddling along a stream, I would suddenly see far ahead of me a great shape slide off the bank with a splash, and the watchful old alligator would have disappeared. That their hearing is very acute is proven by the fact that it is almost impossible to walk up on an alligator while it is on the bank, or if it is an old shy individual, to get a glimpse of it by walking to its den. The alligator invariably hears an approaching individual and sinks out of sight long before it can be seen, and long before it could see one approach. It could only tell of an approach by hearing. An alligator hears readily while under the water, and if no alligators are in sight, I frequently bring them to the surface by imitating the cry of a dog or the peculiar grunting sound that a young alligator makes when it has strayed away from its mother.

When taking sunbaths on the bank, it is usual for alligators to hold their mouths partly open. I have never in all my experiences seen them snap their jaws together at such times, although flies and mosquitoes swarm around them. I believe the reason they open their mouths is to let the leeches and small water lice which frequently attach themselves inside of their mouths along the tongue to have a chance to dry out in the hot sunlight, which perhaps would rid them of these pests. I can think of no other reason. I have never seen an alligator swim with its mouth open or partly open.

During the early years after the establishment of the wild life refuges in Louisiana; that is, the Sage Wild Life Refuge, Marsh Island; the Grande Cheniere Tract which is the Rockefeller Foundation Wild Life Refuge; and the Bayou Ferman Tract which is the Ward-McIlhenny Wild Life Refuge; a total of one hundred and seventy-four thousand acres, there was no killing of alligators allowed covering a period of four years. During that time the alligators increased enormously, and the muskrat trappers claimed that they were destroying great numbers of muskrats. During the Summer of 1916, it was decided to reduce the alligators on these refuges, and something over one hundred men were given permits to hunt alligators on them. The total kill during that Summer on these three wild refuges was between eighty-eight thousand and eighty-nine thousand alligators. This is illustrative of how rapidly alligators will increase if left alone.

Mother alligators show the greatest solicitude for their young, both while they are undeveloped in the egg, and after they are hatched. Before alligators had become, by persecution, so very shy of human beings, the mother alligator invariably protected its nest from attack, and it was dangerous for anyone to molest one. I have been witness to very many attacks by alligators on persons who were opening their nests. At present, I believe, generally speaking, alligators are too shy and too much afraid of human beings to attack even if their nests are disturbed. In the few isolated places where they have not been disturbed they will still defend their nests and young. As soon as the young are hatched, they are led by the mother to her den, which is usually in a secluded pool in the wet prairie or at the head of some small bayou. The young remain with, and are guarded by, the mother from the time of hatching all through the Winter, and until the next spring's mating period. At this time the female wanders off in search of a mate, and the young, being then about sixteen or eighteen inches in length and well able to take care of themselves, spread over the surrounding marshes and bayous. I have known young alligators, who had been toe-marked for iden-tification, to leave their mother in the Spring during April and wander more than a mile to inland ponds in a com-paratively few days after leaving the home den.

Large male alligators are very intolerant of the near ap-proach to the place in which they live, of other large males, and I think most of the roaring they do is for the purpose of warning away any other who might invade their range. The males fight each other fiercely and it is not uncommon to find large males with a foot or leg missing, or a con-siderable section of its tail gone, or severe scars on its body, which could only be made by other alligators. I have often seen them fighting. They fight only with their mouths, and the only use they make of their tails during a fight is to use it as a lever to get their mouths in better position for biting, or to help them to roll after a jaw-hold has been secured. Sometimes they lock jaws and try their best to twist off each others head by turning over and over sideways as fast as they can. If a hold is gotten on a leg or tail the roll is immediately started with the usual result that the mem-ber grasped is twisted off.

In snapping at a rival, or anything, if the object is missed, the jaws come together with such a force that a loud sound is made, as if two heavy planks had been slapped together.

CHAPTER VIII

NEST AND NEST-BUILDING

There is considerable variation in the size and in the location of alligator nests. Old, fully-grown females will frequently use the same location year after year, building each succeeding nest on top of the old one until quite a mound accumulates. Such a nest may be as much as ten feet across the base and four feet in height at the centre. This does not mean that the nest is built this large each year, but the new nest being built on top of the old nest year after year, and the old nest having been spread or mashed down somewhat before the new nest is built, the size above stated is sometimes reached. The usual size of an alligator's nest is about five to seven feet at the base, with a two and one-half to three foot cone; but I have found nests that were very much smaller than this containing a full complement of eggs. Alligators lay only once in a season and deposit all of their eggs at one time in an irregular mass, without any material being placed between the eggs. After the eggs are laid in the hollow of the nest, (which hollow is made after the nest is built by digging the top out with the hind feet,) they are covered by the alligator's taking the loose material needed for covering them in its mouth and dropping it on top of the eggs, crawling backwards and forwards across the covering material to firm it down. The nest is always cone-shaped—some much more pointed than others. Sometimes the top of the nest is plastered with mud taken from under the marsh grass roots, and there is usually some mud mixed with the wet material forming the upper part of the nest. In wet weather or after each rain, the mother alligator slides across her nest backward and forward to slick down

A TYPICAL ALLIGATOR'S NEST.

AN ALLIGATOR'S NEST OPENED SHOWING THE EGGS IN PLACE.

the top material that may have been roughed by the action
of the raindrops—this is in order to hold in the heat of the
decaying vegetable matter surrounding the eggs. Should
there be a period of two or three days or more without rain,
the old alligator crawls over the nest and evacuates a considerable amount of water on top of the nest so as to keep
the nest-material wet and the eggs damp. This wetting
down is done with great regularity each day or night during periods of drought.

There is considerable variation in the number of eggs
laid by an alligator. Of the hundreds of nests I have
opened, twenty-nine is the smallest number of eggs found;
sixty-eight the largest. My chief warden, Lionel LeBlanc,
reports opening an alligator's nest in the marshes just back
of Cheniere au Tigre in Vermilion Parish several years
ago that contained eighty-eight eggs. He is very positive
in his statement that he counted these eggs personally, and
as they were all approximately the same size, he is sure
they were the clutch of one alligator.

Alligators build their nests and lay their eggs from the
twentieth of May to the twenty-fifth of June. I have never
found a nest with freshly laid eggs in it earlier than May
twentieth, nor later than June twenty-fifth. The first two
weeks of June would cover the bulk of the laying season.

It is generally supposed by those that have written on
the alligator, that the period of incubation of alligator eggs
is eight weeks. The normal incubation period is nine weeks.
I have tested this time and again with always the same re-
sults, within one or two days; sometimes one day less, sometimes two days more.

The nests of alligators are robbed for their eggs by
'coons, opossums, bears, hogs, and, of course, man. The
first four named, eat the eggs, but I have never known alligator eggs to be used by humans for food, although there
is no reason why they should not be as palatable as turtle
eggs.

The flesh of the tail of the young alligator is excellent, although it is not eaten generally, even by the natives, except a few who are not especially squeamish about their food. I have often eaten it fried, roasted, fricasseed, and finely chopped and baked. When properly cooked and seasoned, it is as good flesh as I want to eat, and should be universally used for food. Its taste resembles somewhat whale or porpoise meat, having a slight, fishy taste. Resembling, however, in both taste and texture, meat rather than fish.

The following nesting records are of value in the life history of this creature, and speak for themselves.

I have for many years kept alligators in large pens built on the edge of my wild life refuge on Avery Island, Louisiana. At first these pens were about thirty feet square, build by driving two by ten-inch cypress plank five feet into the pond's bottom and extending above the water line for about five feet, taking in both bank and water. There were three of these pens with connecting doors between them. In two of the pens I kept large male alligators, in the third a large female. At the proper time for several years the female was turned in with a male, and after mating put back to her pen, where she for four years built a nest on the bank from material furnished her, usually hay and fresh cut marsh grass; laid a clutch of eggs which in due time were hatched. I kept annually a close record of the nest building and time of incubation, but as this procedure was somewhat artificial, I, in order to get accurate nesting data on these big reptiles under perfectly normal conditions, on May 26, 1921, turn a large female, who measured nine feet, one inch, in with a nine foot male. They had shown a desire to get together for several days, and the male had been unusually noisy, roaring at frequent intervals day and night.

As soon as the connecting door was opened the female went through to the male, and without preliminary maneu-

HEARING THE YOUNG ONES GRUNTING, I OPENED THE NEST AND FOUND
SOME OF THE EGGS NOT YET HATCHED.

vers they at once mated. Mating was accomplished in the
water by the male mounting the back of the female, taking
her firmly around the body with front and back feet; the
female turned a little to one side raised her tail turning it
sidewise, the male's tail being turned sidewise and under her; the mating act was accomplished. Copulation oc-
curred often during the next three days, each act lasting
between ten to fifteen minutes. Then the pair showing
no further interest in each other, the female was put back
in her pen and the door closed.

On June 3, a couple of planks between the female's pen
and the outside pond were taken off and she was allowed to
go free.

The pond, on the edge of which my alligator pens are
built, is an artificial one, about five hundred feet from my
house, made by damming the outlet to a little valley. It
contains about thirty-five acres of water, varying in depth
from a few inches to ten feet, in and over which there is a
thick growth of swamp-loving trees and shrubs and much
saw grass, lotus and other water-growing plants. It is in
this pond, "Bird City," established many years ago, that
I have my Egret and Heron colony, and a large variety of
other water and marsh-loving birds nest here. The water
of the pond teems with fish, turtles and snakes, and
along its banks are numerous muskrat nests. This pond is
an ideal alligator home, as everything needed by these great
reptiles is there in abundance.

Every morning after the female's release, I had a man
go around the pond to locate the place where she would
make her nest. On June 19, it was reported to me that
an alligator was clearing a place on the bank, and I at once
went to investigate. I found the liberated female busily at
work in a brier patch on the north side of the pond, about
thirty feet back from the water on high dry ground. She
had mashed a road down through the briers and small
bushes by crawling over them from the water's edge to the

point where she had started her nest. When I got near the
spot, she was making considerable noise biting off the growth
and making a clearing. On seeing me she hurried down
her road and disappeared into the water. Realizing that
in order to observe the nest building I must be hidden; I
with some assistance, as quietly as possible made a small
opening through the thicket that would give me a clear
view of the alligator's road to the water and the opening
in which nest building was just beginning, and about fifteen
feet from where it was evident the nest was to be built.
Across this opening I placed on sticks driven in the ground
a piece of burlap forming three sides of a square through
which peep-holes were cut, masking this blind from the nest
side with green bamboo tops. Behind this blind I had a
box placed to sit on, and then left the vicinity. About
two hours later I quietly went to the blind, and while I was
still quite a long way from the observation place, was
thrilled to hear the alligator at work. Reaching my box
seat and looking through the camouflaged lookout I could
plainly see the work of nest-building, and it proved much
more elaborate than I had suspected.

When I started watching, this alligator had probably not
been at work for more than three or four hours, perhaps
three hours before I built the blind, and certainly not more
than one hour later, but she had bitten off and mashed
down all vegetation over a space about ten feet by eight
feet, and had gathered a lot of the material into a rough
pile near the centre of her clearing. When I first saw her
at work she was scooping up, from the outside edges of her
trash pile, in her mouth, twigs and leaves, and holding them
firmly, would back across the center of the pile dropping
her burden on top of the mound already of considerable
size in width and height. She would then go forward and
get another mouthful from the outside edge of her clearing and pull it across and past the centre. This pulling of
the brush and trash from the outside past the centre con-

tinued until she had made the circle of the pile four and
one-half times, which required almost five hours work. In
making this part of the clearing four Alder trees, from two
and one-half to three inches in diameter, had been broken
off. When these were pulled onto the pile, their trunks
were found too large for nest building, so she laid her body
across the trunks and tore off the limbs by crushing them
in her jaws and with violent shakes of her head. After the
limbs were stripped off, the trunks were carried by mouth
to the side of the clearing and discarded. Occasionally she
would go to the edge of the cleared space and turning her
head sidewise would grasp in her jaws a mouthful of whatever the standing growth might be, and after crushing the
stems so caught by strongly squeezing her jaws together,
would start backing towards the nest, dragging with her
whatever material her jaws held, thus tearing the weaker
stems off or up by the roots, and breaking off by violent
shakes of her head such stems as were too strong to be gotten loose otherwise. When this part of the nest-building
had been finished, the result was a pile of stems, twigs and
leaves, almost round, and about six feet across by about
eighteen inches high. By continually crawling over this
mound and working its material from the edge to the centre
it was well packed and flat on top. The nest-builder then
left off work and went back to the pond, and I also called
it a day.

The next morning I was at the nest-blind before sunrise,
provided with a lunch and a jug of water, prepared to spend
the day. The alligator was not at the nest and did not
come to work until 7:35, but when it got light enough to
see clearly, I found the nest-building had continued during
the night, as the cleared space was considerably larger, and
a lot of loose twigs, leaves, briers and dry trash had been
piled loosely around the base of the nest-mound. Arriving
at the mound, the alligator looked it over holding her head
as high as possible while slowly crawling around its base.

She then crawled on top and at once began nest-building in a most expert and methodical manner. Lying across the nest pile, tail on one side, head on the other, she would reach down catching the loose material, and the projecting material which she had loosely piled at the base of the mound, in her mouth, and holding it firmly, back across the nest bringing the material across the center to the opposite top side where it was deposited and firmed down as the weight of her body was pushed forward across it to the edge again. This work continued until two complete circles of the nest had been made, and it was raised at least ten inches higher; this work occupied two hours and twenty minutes of time. She, now being apparently satisfied with the height of her nest, crawled down and went slowly around it, head held high, looking intently at the shape of the sides, but paying most attention to the top. Being satisfied with its appearance, she now went to the top of the mound and placing her hind feet near the centre, lay flat, bracing her front feet into the outside edge of the nest-material, she then began drawing up and pushing back her hind feet slowly one at a time and turning slowly around the rim of the mound. This action pushed the twigs and leaves from the center towards the outside rim of the mound, and after a couple of circles of the mound had been made in this manner, the center was decidedly hollow, and the outside edges seemed raised at least ten to twelve inches above the center. This was plainly shown by the curve of the alligator's body as she worked out the depression. After two hours and forty-five minutes of this work the nest-builder slid down the side of the nest and without hesitation made her way to the water.

It was now a few minutes after one o'clock, and I supposed she had "knocked off" work for lunch, but I was afraid to leave as something might happen in the nest-building during my absence. From time to time I could hear considerable noise in the rushes in the pond which

I thought was made by the alligator, but was entirely un-
prepared for what I was next to see; which was, what looked
like a bushel of wet and muddy rushes suddenly appearing
in the water at the beginning of the alligator's path to the
nest. This mass of material advanced steadily up the path,
but it was not until it reached the nest-clearing that I could
see that the alligator was carrying a huge mouthful of
rushes and their roots and the mud in which they grew.
This mass completely hid her head as she advanced up the
nest-road. Coming to the nest-mound she crawled up to
the top and deposited the mouthful of wet material in the
hollow of the nest. With only a short pause, back to the
pond she went, and I could plainly hear her tearing at the
growing rushes. In about ten minutes she reappeared with
another large mouthful of the same sort of material which
she also put in the depression at the top of the nest. The
work of bringing wet rushes and mud from the pond to
the nest and filling the hollowed-out top continued for three
hours and fifteen minutes, and nine trips were made to the
pond and back to the nest. By this time the hollow in the
top had been filled with this wet material until it was considerably higher than the sides. She then climbed down
and walked all around the mound then back to the top, and
scooped up material with her mouth from places that did
not suit her fancy, placing it on other parts of the top, all
the while moving slowly round and round over and back
of the nest's top (which was by now at least three feet
high) until quite a regular hay-stack-like cone was shaped.
It was now ten minutes after six. I kept watch until 7:30,
and as it was then too dark to see more, called it a day.

I was in my blind before sunrise the next morning, and
as soon as it was light enough to see, observed the nest and
surroundings were exactly as they were the night before.
I saw nothing of her until ten minutes after ten o'clock,
when she came to the point where her path to the nest joined
the water, but did not come out of the water until 11:40.

She came slowly up the path to the nest, went part way round it, then climbed on top, and putting her head and forepart over the southern edge and her tail pointing north, began hollowing out the center with her hind feet, pushing the wet material from the center to the sides by drawing her hind feet alternately forward and pushing them back and down with considerable force, turning her body about the rim of the nest as the hollow progressed. This hollow was not made as wide as the first hollow, but was deeper, and as it was in softer material, much more quickly made.

At 12:35 P.M., she placed her hind legs on each side of the hollow and began at once depositing her eggs. The eggs were laid quite rapidly and regularly at first, as near as I could time, one every nine seconds. As the eggs were deposited the alligator turned slowly, the center part of her body following irregularly the inside rim of the nest-hollow, forward and back. I could not keep an accurate count of the eggs laid, as I was too busy timing the operation and making notes, but when about thirty eggs had been laid, there was a pause of sixteen minutes, during which time she kept quiet and relaxed. Then straightening up somewhat, she began to drop eggs; after six had been laid she again paused, and after seven minutes rest laid five more. Then rested quietly for eight minutes, then pushed her body to one side of the top of the nest, taking a large mouthful of wet mashed rushes and trash from the side rim of the nest where it had been pushed from the center while making the hollow to contain her eggs, she dropped the mouthful on top of the eggs, and continued doing this until the cavity in which the eggs lay was filled to the top with the wet mixture of broken rushes and trash. The old alligator then slid down the edge of the nest, went to the pond, and I could hear her pulling and tearing at the growing rushes. In a few minutes back to the nest she came with a large mouthful of broken rushes and material from below the surface of the water and dropped it on top of the nest as

I WAS STARTLED BY HEARING A LOUD HISS AND THERE WAS THE MOTHER ALLIGATOR MAKING FOR ME WITH MOUTH OPENED.

she came up one side, then deliberately slid her body across the top of the nest, turned and slid back so that the whole weight of her body pressed the wet material down on the eggs. She then went to the pond again, and after tearing at the rushes a couple of minutes came out with another mixed mouthful which she deposited on top of the nest, crawling over it as before. Six trips were made for broken green rushes, mud and the partly decayed material from below the water, all of which was placed on the top of the nest. As the center-fill got higher, she crawled around the slope of the cone-like top instead of crawling over the top. This caused the top to be quite pointed, very much like a small round top hay-stack, and very smooth, as the weight of her body slicked the mud and rushes together like smooth plaster. She then slid down to the ground, crawled around the nest, slowly inspecting it, then went down her road to the pond. It was now ten minutes after four, and although I waited in the blind until six-thirty, she did not come back.

The next morning I went to the blind at sunrise, but saw no signs of the old one's having been at the nest. After waiting a couple of hours I went to the nest with a tape line to take some measurements. As I stood looking at it, I was startled by hearing a loud hiss, and turning, there was the mother alligator at the edge of her road at the water; her head and fore-parts on the bank, mouth half open, and showing by her expression great resentment at my nearness to her nest. I went about taking the measurements of the nest and she came out of the water to within a few feet of me, mouth part-way open and hissing loudly and often. I went quietly about my measuring clucking to her soothingly, and she quieted down, but kept near the nest, and I feel sure had I attempted to molest the nest she would have attacked me. Having completed what I wanted, I withdrew to my blind to watch. The old alligator being satisfied I had left, slowly crawled around her nest, then went to the water and kept watch with her head on the bank, keeping this position for about thirty minutes, then slowly backed out of sight into the rushes. Although I kept watch for another thirty minutes, she did not come in sight again. The finished nest measured seven feet, two inches across the base, three feet, four inches high to the top of the cone. Its base was round and the nest tapered regularly from the base of a rounded cone, shaped like the blunt end of a hen's egg.

Many times in the following days I visited the nest and always found the old one on guard; or she appeared shortly after my arrival, ready to defend her nest against molestation. If I made as if to disturb the nest she would come out of the water as fast as she could with mouth half open and hissing loudly, and I would always have to retreat, for she showed every intention of attacking.

During the period of incubation, there was no material added to the nest, but on the days when it did not rain, the old alligator would crawl over the top of the nest and liberally wet it by voiding water through her vent in order to keep the nest-material and the eggs moist. On very hot, dry days this wetting was done twice a day. After a hard rain she would crawl on top of the nest and drag her body over it, thus slicking the surface, I suppose to better hold the inside heat (of the decaying vegetable matter of which the nest was composed) around the eggs. Towards the end of the eighth week after she laid her eggs, I visited the nest twice daily, as I knew by past experience that the eggs should hatch in about sixty days. On August 21, I could plainly hear the young ones grunting in the nest, and knew they must be hatching, but as the mother had not opened the nest, I did not disturb it. She seemed more than ever anxious at my being near the nest and showed by her repeatedly coming at me that she would attack if I attempted to molest her nursery. I knew the young would not come out of the nest until she had removed the top six or eight inches, so I went to my blind to keep watch. The

THE FEMALE ALLIGATOR GUARDS HER NEST AGAINST ENEMIES.

old one, after crawling a couple of times around her nest
and finding all well, went back to the water at the end of
the path; keeping in sight of the nest. I watched her all
day, but she did not again go to the nest. (I may state
here that a female alligator guards her nest against enemies; keeping constantly near it to protect it from de-
struction by 'coons, opossums, bears and hogs; all these
animals eat alligator eggs if they get the chance. When
the young begin hatching, they make the fact known to
their mother by a shrill, grunting sound. The old alligator
then removes with her mouth the packed-down material
covering the hatching little ones, so that they can crawl out
of the nest and join her. If she did not open the nest, the
young would be held prisoners by the tightly packed material over them, and eventually starve to death. I have
opened alligators' nests, from five to seven months after the
young had hatched, and found the little alligators alive,
but unable to get through the nest-material surrounding
them. The female alligators to whom these nests belonged
had probably been killed by hide-hunters. The young after
hatching stay with their mother until the next Spring.)

Next morning, August 22, I was at the nest very early
and found the mother had bitten off the top material, for
about ten inches deep, and thrown it to the side of the nest
away from the water. The young could be heard giving
their baby call of "umph-umph-umph," which sound can be
exactly imitated by the human voice if the syllable is pronounced with the mouth closed and in a high key. Knowing that as soon as the full heat of the day came, the young
would leave the nest, and wishing to measure, weigh and
mark them, I got one of my men, a basket, rope, tape-line
and postal scales, and was back at the nest in a very short
time. As soon as we went up to the nest the mother came
at us with mouth open, hissing loudly. I dropped a noose
over her head, tied her to a willow tree on the edge of the
water, where after a few tugs and rolls she became quiet,

except for hissing at us, and we proceeded to remove the
two or three inches of loose nest-material from over the
little alligators. As I expected, all the eggs were hatched
and the young as pretty and lively as could be. They were
put into a basket, and a hollow was made in the center of the
nest down to the hard ground so that they could be put
back into the nest after I was through with them. Every
egg had hatched and there were forty-two of the little
fellows. They measured from eight and one-half to nine
and one-half inches, none more, none less. Their weight
was from two and one-eighth to two and seven-
eighths ounces. All of them had on the top end of the
upper jaw a very small thorn-like point, evidently for the
purpose of scratching a hole through the tough inner egg
covering. After all had been measured and weighed I put
them back in the basket, and marked them by cutting the
first joint off one or more toes and splitting the web between one or more toes for future identification, making a
record of each mark. The hollow in the nest was then
partly filled, the young put back and covered over loosely
with the material that had been taken from over them, and
after freeing the mother and giving her a few pieces of raw
meat, which she readily took, I left the nest, made around
quietly and got into my blind and saw that the old alligator
was crawling around the nest making low grunts, sounding
very much like a large pig, and the young could be heard
answering. She slowly went down her path to the water
grunting every little while. On reaching the water, she
turned keeping her head on land towards the nest, but with
most of her body in the water. At 11:30 the first of the
young pushed through the loose top covering and it was
quickly followed by the others; all of them ran in a most
lively way to the mother who kept her position and continued to grunt. Her little ones took to the water along-
side her and she slowly backed out of sight into the rushes
with them on each side and following.

Every three or four days after the young alligators were hatched I would go to the edge of the pond near the old nest with some chunks of raw meat, and give the popping call which all alligators seem to understand—means "come," and she would come for her food, but she never brought her young with her.

On September 20, just twenty-nine days after the young alligators were hatched, I thought I would find the old one's den and measure some of the young. Taking a long bamboo pole, to the end of which I had attached a telephone line wire, bent to form an inverted V with the angle somewhat round and the free point flaired out sharply, and which I thought would serve as well to catch little alligators, as it did to catch herons by the legs while tagging them, and putting on a pair of hip-boots, I waded into the marsh through water about one to two feet deep to the spot from which the old alligator always came when I called her for food. Walking very quietly, I came to an opening in the grass and lotus about fifty feet from the bank. This opening was about ten feet long and eight feet wide, and had been made by the old alligator biting and mashing off the plant growth and then waving it clear from the center to the sides with her tail, and then loosening the muck at the bottom of the space cleaned, sweeping it to the sides of the opening with her tail until the clearing was open water about two feet deep, and the sides of it banked several inches above the water with mud and plant stems. At the far end of this opening her head was in sight and around her in the water and on the banks of the opening, quietly sunning themselves, were her young ones. In spite of my quiet approach she heard me, for she was watching intently in my direction. As I came through the grass towards her she gave a few low grunts and all the young ones slid off the banks and disappeared under the water. At my nearer approach she raised herself high in the water by inflating her body with air until at least half her body was above the water, and the last foot and one-half of her tail kept rapidly moving from side to side. I kept on slowly towards her, and when about twenty feet from her, she rushed at me through the water with mouth open and with a loud roaring hiss. For about ten feet her approach was very rapid, but her speed quickly slackened and she came to a stop at about six feet from where I stood in water about eighteen inches deep. As I did not move she showed no disposition to attack, but kept puffing herself full of wind and hissing loudly. I kept perfectly still and she gradually quieted down and backed into her den, which I then saw she had dug under a big bunch of saw grass at the far end of the opening. She kept her head sticking out of the hole at the edge of the grass, and as I saw I could not get the young ones by this sort of an approach, I went to the shore, got a skiff, some rope and a man to pole me, and we pushed the boat through the floating grass to the den. As soon as the bow of the skiff got in the open water near her den, she rushed the boat very much as she had rushed me, and grabbing the gunnel in her mouth wrenched off a piece of plank about four inches wide and eight feet long, driving her teeth clear through the almost inch-thick lumber. As I knew, because of her fierceness, I could not get the young while she was at liberty, I dropped a noose of heavy rope over her head, drew her to the stern of the boat; then up until her head was above the boat, with her wide gapping jaws resting on the upper stern plank, and pressing her top jaw down with an oar, caught her two jaws firmly together at the nose with my left hand, and with my right took a couple of half-hitches around her closed jaws, and she was secured and harmless. I then kept quite near the mouth of the den, and after about ten minutes, imitated the mother's assembly call (which is a low, musical umph-umph-umph, given with the mouth closed), at short intervals, and as the young ones came to the surface of the water at the mouth of the den, caught eight of them with my bamboo and wire

SHE RUSHED AT ME WITH MOUTH OPEN.

attachment. I was surprised to find the young ones had increased in length from five to six inches in the twenty-nine days since they left their nest, and now measured from thirteen and one-half inches to fourteen and one-half inches. I did not weigh them.

I had kept four of the young ones, taken the day they hatched, in a pan of water near the kitchen stove at my house, and the largest of these today measured only ten and one-half inches; an increase of only one inch. Clearly showing the young in their natural habitat get more and better nourishment.

From time to time for several years, or until the marked alligators got too large, I would go into the pond at night in a small boat with a man paddling me, an electric head-light on my hat, and a stiff bamboo pole to the end of which was attached a strong wire slip noose, and catch these young alligators, put them in sacks, and the next day measure and weigh them, then turn them loose in the pond again. This data has been carefully kept during the ten years since the young alligators were hatched, and gives a pretty accurate record of the growth of alligators under normal conditions in the wild.

In the late Summer of 1927, these alligators having attained quite a size were worrying the birds, especially the herons, all night long, and I was frequently awakened by the loud closing slap of their jaws as they snapped at the birds in the low trees, and the outcry of the birds as numbers of them in the vicinity of the attack took alarm. I then determined to have a lot of these alligators killed, and on August 26, 1927, had Leonce LeBlanc, one of my men, set a number of quarter-inch lines tied to limbs of trees overhanging the water; to the free end of each was attached a heavy hook baited with a chunk of raw meat, suspended about one foot above the water. In two nights he caught twelve of these alligators, and others have been killed since. A record has been kept of the contents of the stomach of these alligators and is of considerable interest in determining their destructiveness.

It is interesting here to note that on October 3, 1921, I caught the female I had liberated and put her in the pen with the male with whom she had been mated, for the Winter, as I had gotten a large male and put him in her pen during the time she was at liberty. The morning after she was put in with her mate she was found dead. He had killed her during the night. An examination showed he had caught her across the body just back of the front legs in his jaws and squeezed her to death. A few days after the female death I was much surprised to see twenty-eight of her young ones in the pen with an eleven and one-half foot male. These little fellows stayed with this big alligator all Winter. It was amusing to see them on warm, sunny days basking in the sun on top of his back, and often on top of his head. They went into his den in cold weather and he made no attempt to harm them; but they left him in the Spring before he began to eat.

E. A. McILHENNY OPENING AN ALLIGATOR'S NEST.

CHAPTER IX

INCUBATION AND GROWTH OF YOUNG

On the eighteenth of June, 1931, an alligator started building its nest in a large clump of Egyptian Papyrus (Cyperus Papyrus) about fifty feet from shore in my wild life refuge on Avery Island, where I had liberated a lot of toe-marked little alligators in 1921.

The place was easy to get to, but there was no suitable location near the nest to put up an observation blind, so the actual construction of the nest was not watched. This was a young female, one of the lot I had marked for identification August 22, 1921, with her first nest.

The Papyrus growth in which the nest was being built was very thick, about ten feet high, growing in about eight inches of water on the edge of deep water and close against a concrete, retaining wall. These heavy, soft-stemmed plants were mashed down at the location for the nest, by the alligator crawling over them. When I first saw the spot on June 18, at 8:30 A.M., a clearing had been made about eight feet by eight feet, and a considerable number of Papyrus stems had been torn loose and were loosely piled in the center. The nest-builder backed into the deep water, which was only a few feet from the nest, on my approach, and watched me, but showed no fear.

At noon on the nineteenth, the nest was about two feet above the water, and as far as I could see, built entirely of the stems of Papyrus. At noon on the twentieth, the nest was two feet, ten inches above the water with a six foot, four inch base. The top part was now covered with grass roots, mud and decaying vegetation taken from below the water. At noon on the twenty-first, the nest was apparently finished. It had been raised a little higher but the top had not been coned and slicked down, so I knew the eggs had not been deposited. Nothing was done to the nest on the twenty-second. The eggs had not been laid at eight o'clock in the morning of the twenty-third, but the alligator was on the nest and had begun to hollow the center. At noon on the twenty-third, the eggs had been laid, the nest coned with trash and mud taken from below the water surface and slicked down. At two o'clock on the afternoon of the twenty-third, I, with a couple of men, went to the nest, dropped a noose over the head of the alligator when she came out on the nest to defend it; measured the nest which was three feet, nine inches in height, eight inches being in water with a seven foot base; measured and weighed the eggs which averaged 2.61 inches long by 1.60 inches through, and weighed an average of two and one-eighth ounces; counted the eggs which numbered thirty-four; placed a double registering thermometer with its bulb at the center of the eggs slanted so that its top was six inches below the top of the nest-material; recovered the eggs and thermometer, firming down the nest-material so that the nest was exactly as it had been; measured the mother alligator who was seven feet, three inches; turned her loose and departed.

This alligator is one of the lot of young, hatched August 22, 1921, and easily identified by the toe-marks made and recorded when it was liberated. This was her first nest, and the first nest made by any of the lot. It is of interest here to note that the first nesting of this lot of alligators was nine years and ten months after hatching, and this under perfectly normal conditions.

During the incubation period this nest was visited almost daily and an exact record made of the maximum and minimum temperature of the nest at the eggs, and a corresponding record of the outside temperature in the shade. A record was also kept of the rainfall. The data thus gathered gives a very clear picture of the incubating temperature of an alligator's nest and the development of the embryo under normal conditions.

Some writers state that in alligator's eggs, embryonic development starts before the eggs are deposited in the nest. This I have not found to be a fact, and I have examined the fresh eggs from very many alligators' nests, also the fully-developed eggs taken from many freshly-killed alligators. The one egg opened from this nest the day laid was without sign of embryonic development. It is possible that should an alligator be kept from laying at the proper time that her eggs should be laid, due to drouth or other unusual causes, that she will retain the eggs for a time in her body, and under such conditions embryonic development would start before the eggs are deposited in the nest. I have seen this very thing in the eggs of fresh-water turtles, when the turtles were kept during the laying season for a considerable time on hard surface in which they could make no nests, and therefore retained in their bodies eggs for several weeks past the time when they should have been laid. The embryos in such abnormally retained eggs begin development in the parent, but if the eggs are retained too long the embryonic deveopment ceases and the entire inside of the egg becomes a tough, yellow mass. If embryonic development has been found in the eggs of alligators while retained in the mother, it should be considered an unusual occurrence and due to irregular causes. Having examined fresh eggs from hundreds of alligator nests, and the eggs taken from hundreds of freshly-killed alligators without ever finding embryonic development in such eggs, I make the above statement with great positiveness.

The following temperature records of this alligator's nest taken with the bulb of the thermometer set at the center of the egg clutch is, I believe, the first such record. It is of interest to note that following rain the nest's temperature was usually lowered. On days when there was no rain the mother would liberally wet down the top of the nest in order to prevent evaporation and the drying-out of the nest-material.   There were ten and one-half inches of material above the top of the eggs and much more than this around the sides of the eggs.   The eggs were laid in an irregular mass with none of the material from which the nest was built between them.   I have opened hundreds of alligator nests and have never found the eggs deposited in layers with a covering of the nest-material between them.

DATE 1931	TEMPERATURE IN NEST		OUTSIDE TEMPERATURE IN SHADE		RAINFALL IN 100 OF INCH	REMARKS
	max.	min.	max.	min.		
June 24	102	100	95	75		The eggs were laid between 9 A.M. and 12 noon, June 23
" 25	102	100	95	76		
" 26	102	100	87	77		
" 27	102	100	82	77		
" 28	102	100	86	78	.63	
July 2	99	96	96	77		Opened one of the eggs; found embryo but slightly developed
" 3	99	96	97	78		
" 4	99	96	97	77		
" 5	98	96	93	78		
" 6	98	95	92	76		
" 12	96	93	89	76	.25	
" 13	96	93	90	79		
" 14	96	93	81	76	.72	
" 21	95	92	92	83		
" 22	95	92	93	76	.06	
" 23	95	92	93	77		
" 24	95	92	92	76		
" 28	95	92	95	77		
" 29	90	90	87	77	.82	
" 30	95	92	89	74		
" 31	95	92	94	76		
Aug. 1	92	90	86	76	.42	*Opened one of the eggs (see (*) next page).
" 2	94	92	88	75	.18	
" 3	94	92	88	76		
" 4	94	92	95	78		
" 5	94	92	95	76		
" 6	94	92	93	76		
" 7	94	91	92	77		
" 8	93	88	92	77	.50	
" 9	93	91	91	78		
" 10	92	91	93	78	.14	
" 11	92	89	97	75		
" 12	92	89	87	66		
" 13	92	88	87	66		

" 14	92	86	•	88	66	
" 16	92	84		88	68	**Opened one of the eggs (see **).
" 20	93	88	83	76	.32	
" 21	92	86	83	74		
" 22	92	86	82	74		
" 23	92	86	83	71		***The hard shell on the egg (see (***) next page).
" 24	92	86	83	71		
" 25	92	86	85	73		
" 26	92	86	82	75	.46	
" 27	92	86	87	73		
" 28	—	—	—	—		****Young hatching today—(see (****) next page).
" 29	—	—	—	—		Young left the nest last night.

*Opened one of the eggs, found the little alligator well developed, fully shaped and fully colored, with black and yellow markings as distinct as if naturally hatched. A considerable amount of the yolk was yet to be absorbed. The girth of the eggs is somewhat enlarged, and the hard outside shell is cracked and spread in many places showing the inside membrane.

**Opened one of the eggs today, the little alligator is fully developed, it can see and opened its mouth when my finger was put near it. The circumference of the eggs has increased, and the outer hard shell is much cracked with two openings extending irregularly from end to end showing the tough inner covering of the embryo. The young alligator has a sharp point on the top of its upper jaw, pointing up. This point looks like the point on the beak of a young chicken when first hatched, and is undoubtedly for the purpose of puncturing the tough inner shell at the time of hatching. All the egg's liquid except about one-half a tablespoon of the yolk had been absorbed. There was an opening in the skin of the stomach just forward of the vent one and five-eighths inches long. The stomach membrane protrudes from this opening, and surrounds the remaining yolk. The stomach is quite distended. This little alligator moved its body very slowly due to the distended stomach. This little alligator was placed in a pan containing a couple of inches of tepid water and kept in my house. In six days the yolk had all been absorbed, the stomach opening closed and it was as normal as if it had not had a premature birth.

The thorn on the point of the upper jaw disappeared on the seventh day.

***The hard shell on the eggs is now cracked all over, the eggs are much swollen with the hard outer shell crumbling off. The inner flexible shell is also getting soft and flaky and seems to be considerably thickened and disintegrating.

****The young alligators could be plainly heard grunting in the nest last evening, and this morning when I visited the nest the top material had been bitten off and thrown to one side, the recording thermometer with it, and the head and shoulders of a little alligator was pushed through the loose covering left on the top. On removing this loose covering a number of the newly-hatched, little ones could be seen, also some unhatched eggs. Eight of the little ones were toe-marked, measured and weighed for future reference, put back in the nest and covered up as it was found. All these little ones had a minute, sharp point on the end of the nose. The mother was very uneasy all the time I was handling her young, and it was necessary to have two men with heavy wooden pitch-forks constantly watching to keep her from getting to me. The young measured from eight and one-half inches to eight and seven-eighths inches in length, and weighed one and one-half ounces to two ounces. On the morning of the twenty-ninth, I visited the nest and found all the little ones had left.

This nest of alligator eggs took sixty-six days to hatch, several days longer than the average, which is from sixty-two to sixty-four days. This delay in hatching was probably due to two causes. First, the outside temperature chart shows the weather was cooler than usual for this section of Louisiana. Second, in opening the nest almost daily (although the opening was only about three inches square and closed as soon as the thermometer was read) it is possible the nest temperature was reduced slightly. The outside temperature did not seem to effect the inside nest temperature, and on some days the outside shade temperature was greater than the nest temperature, as on August fourth and fifth, nest temperature ninety-four degrees; outside temperature ninety-five degrees. August eleventh, nest temperature ninety-two degrees, outside ninety-seven degrees.

The foregoing is a record of a normal nesting of an alligator, and I have observed a very great many such nestings, and have always been convinced that the method of nest-building employed by alligators (that is the using of green plant material mixed with mud and partly decayed vegetation) was for the purpose of creating a proper and even temperature in which the embryo would develop. A most unusual nesting came under my observation during the Summer of 1933, which confirms this supposition.

On June 7, 1933, an alligator started scraping together some dry leaves and dry earth on top of a small point extending from my experimental planting garden into the water garden on the north side of my Wild Life Refuge. No grass or wet material was in the pile which was about three inches high, on dry ground, when I first saw it. On the eighth, a number of eggs was deposited in a slight hollow in the loose material, the eggs lying on the hard ground, and when I saw the nest about eight o'clock on the eighth, the top covering of the eggs was so light that a portion of some of them could be seen. At 10:30, the morning of the ninth, about ten inches of dry earth scooped up by the alligator's jaws from near the nest had been placed on top of the eggs, the nest then measured fourteen inches high and thirty-eight inches across. This nest was visited every few days and it was noted that the mother took care of her nest, for after each rain the top was slicked down by her crawling over it, and on dry days the top was made wet as was usual. On August 7, I, thinking it was about time for the eggs to hatch, made a small opening in the nest, took out one of the eggs, and on opening it was surprised to find the embryo only about two-thirds developed. A second egg was then opened with the same result. I was much surprised at the smallness of the embryo as the eggs should have hatched in from two to six days longer, it being sixty days since they were laid. On trying to determine the cause of the slow embryonic development, I noticed there was no grass or leaves or other organic matter used in building the nest and that the eggs were in a solid bed of fairly dry earth. The nest was visited after, and I noticed the mother ceased visiting the nest on August 14, she, evidently, believing the time for hatching had passed. On August 31, I again opened the nest and opened a couple of the eggs, finding the embryos about three-fourths developed, and a large amout of the white and yolk yet to be absorbed. The little alligators were apparently normal and when removed from the eggs could see, and would open their mouths when my finger was put near their heads. I closed the nest and did not open it again until September 22, when while standing near it I thought I heard the grunt of a little alligator. The first egg I uncovered had the head of the little one sticking through the shell and as soon as the egg was lifted from its packed position, the little alligator scrambled out in a lively manner. I then uncovered all of the eggs, and from the thirty-one left in the nest, eight little alligators popped out as soon as the eggs were released from their packed position. In the rest of the eggs the young were fully developed, but dead. The reason that these eggs hatched forty-three days after they should have hatched, was due to the fact that they had had no artificial heat to stimulate embryonic development, as no green plant-material had been used in the nest-building.

On August 22, 1921, I weighed, measured, toe-marked and liberated thirty-eight newly-hatched, little alligators from the nest, the building of which was described in chapter eight. My object in marking and liberating them was to procure accurate data on the growth of alligators under normal conditions. This data was easily gotten by going into the open water of the Refuge in a boat at night and catching the alligators by the light of an electric headlight and with a heavy wire noose on the end of a stiff bamboo pole.

The following data gives an accurate record of their growth and proves conclusively one thing—that alligators, under normal conditions in the wild, grow much more rapidly than is generally supposed, and that both males and females average a little more than one foot increase in length per year up to and including the fifth year, and this increase in length-growth is continued by the males at least to the ninth year, but after the fifth year the females increase in length much more slowly.

These alligators whose age, weights and measurements are here recorded, were liberated at or near the place from which they were caught up to August 26, 1927; those recorded on that date and thereafter were killed, except the female taken June 23, 1931, who was liberated to guard her nest.

DATE	LENGTH	WEIGHT	REMARKS
ug. 22, 1921	9 to 9½ in.	2⅛ to 3 ozs.	Of the 42 young hatched, 38 were liberated with their mother after being marked
pt. 20, 1921	13½ to 14½ in.	. . . .	Eight young were measured to-day.
ne 17, 1922	17¾ in.	8½ ozs.	
ug. 22, 1922	2 ft. 2½ in.	4 lbs. 1 oz.	
ov. 8, 1922	2 ft. 8 in.	5 lbs. 3 ozs.	
" " "	2 ft. 3 in.	4 lbs. 4 ozs.	
" " "	2 ft. 5½ in.	4 lbs. 6 ozs.	
ril 12, 1923	2 ft. 5½ in.	3 lbs. 1 oz.	Very thin, 16 leeches in mouth.
ay 2, 1923	2 ft. 8¼ in.	4 lbs. 1 oz.	
" " "	2 ft. 7½ in.	3 lbs. 9 ozs.	
" " "	2 ft. 7 in.	3 lbs. 10¼ ozs.	
pt. 10, 1923	3 ft. 3 in.	9 lbs. 9½ ozs.	
" " "	3 ft. 4½ in.	10 lbs. 6½ ozs.	
" " "	3 ft. 5½ in.	10 lbs. 4 ozs.	
" " "	3 ft. 11 in.	12 lbs. 7 ozs.	
" " "	3 ft. 9½ in.	11 lbs. 8 ozs.	
ril 13, 1924	3 ft. 8 in.	9 lbs. 4 ozs.	
" " "	3 ft. 8½ in.	9 lbs. 7 ozs.	
" " "	3 ft. 4½ in.	8 lbs. 5 ozs.	
" " "	3 ft. 9 in.	10 lbs.	
" " "	3 ft. 7 in.	8 lbs. 1 oz.	
ct. 3, 1924	4 ft. 3 in.	17 lbs. 4 ozs.	
" " "	4 ft. 6½ in.	17 lbs. 11 ozs.	
" " "	4 ft. 9 in.	19 lbs. 1 oz.	

" " "	4 ft. 2 in.	17 lbs. 4 ozs.
" " "	4 ft. 11 in.	21 lbs. 1½ oz.
June 13, 1925	4 ft. 3½ in.	16 lbs. 9½ ozs.
" " "	3 ft. 10½ in.	11 lbs. 2½ ozs.
" " "	4 ft. 5½ in.	15 lbs. 8 ozs.
" " "	5 ft. 8 in.	29 lbs. 4 ozs.
" " "	4 ft. 3½ in.	16 lbs. 2 ozs.
" " "	4 ft. 4½ in.	16 lbs. 9 ozs.
" " "	4 ft. 3½ in.	16 lbs. 7½ ozs.
" " "	4 ft. 7½ in.	17 lbs. 1 oz.
Oct. 10, 1925	4 ft. 7 in.	19 lbs. 8 ozs.
" " "	5 ft. 2 in.	22 lbs. 11 ozs.
" " "	5 ft. 6½ in.	27 lbs. 6 ozs.
" " "	5 ft. 1 in.	26 lbs. 9 ozs.
" " "	5 ft. 9¾ in.	38 lbs. 10 ozs.

DATE	LENGTH	WEIGHT	SEX	CONTENTS OF STOMACH
Aug. 26, 1927	5 ft. 6 in.	30 lbs.	Fem.	4 herons, 2 garfish.
" " "	5 ft. 9 in.	36 lbs. 8 ozs.	Fem.	5 herons, 1 garfish, 1 turtle.
" " "	5 ft. 7 in.	37 lbs. 2 ozs.	Fem.	4 herons, 1 turtle.
" " "	5 ft. 8 in.	38 lbs. 1 oz.	Fem.	7 herons, 2 turtles.
Aug. 29, 1927	6 ft. 7 in.	69 lbs. 4 ozs.	Male	8 herons, 1 turtle, 1 garfish.
" " "	5 ft. 9 in.	43 lbs. 7 ozs.	Male	7 herons, 1 snake, 1 garfish.
" " "	5 ft. 4 in..	36 lbs. 8 ozs.	Fem.	4 herons, 2 garfish.
" " "	5 ft. 9 in.	41 lbs. 8 ozs.	Male	5 herons, 3 garfish.
" " "	7 ft. 10 in.	124 lbs. 8 ozs.	Male	9 herons, 1 turtle, 2 garfish.
" " "	5 ft. 6 in.	41 lbs.	Fem.	3 herons, 1 rabbit, 1 garfish.
" " "	6 ft. 4½ in.	62½ lbs.	Male	5 herons, 1 snake.
" " "	5 ft. 3½ in.	33 lbs.	Fem.	2 herons, 1 muskrat, 1 snake.
Aug. 20, 1930	6 ft. 10 in.	84½ lbs.	Fem.	5 herons, 1 turtle, 1 snake.
" " "	8 ft. 1 in.	126 lbs.	Male	8 herons, 2 small turtles.
" " "	7 ft. 8½ in.	126½ lbs.	Male	10 herons, 1 turtle, 1 snake.
" " "	8 ft. 4 in.	134 lbs.	Male	4 herons, 3 turtles, 1 garfish.
" " "	8 ft. 9½ in.	149 lbs.	Male	3 herons, 1 garfish, 1 snake.
" " "	6 ft. 7 in.	89 lbs.	Fem.	6 herons, 1 turtle.
June 23, 1931	7 ft. 3 in.	116½ lbs.	Fem.	*Has nest near wall. This the first nest built by the a gators hatched in 1921.
July 29, 1931	8 ft. 10 in.	178 lbs.	Male	4 herons, 1 snake, 1 garfi 2 turtles.
" " "	9 ft. 2 in.	291½ lbs.	Male	7 herons, 2 garfish, 2 turtles.
" " "	9 ft. 5 in.	283 lbs.	Male	5 herons, 4 turtles, 1 snake.
" " "	7 ft. 1½ in.	110 lbs.	Fem.	1 heron, 1 turtle, 1 garfish.
July 15, 1932	8 ft. 8 in.	169 lbs. 8 ozs.	Male	9 herons.
" " "	10 ft. 1 in.	354 lbs.	Male	11 herons, 4 garfish, 4 turtle

This data is interesting from several angles. First, it gives an accurate picture of the normal rate of growth of alligators in the wild state whose ages were definitely known by their having been marked on the day they hatched, and these marks recorded. Second, it shows the difference in growth between males and females of the same age. Third, it shows under identical conditions how similar was the food of the different ones examined. It should be understood that these alligators had been liberated in a wild life refuge in which a great many thousands of herons and other water birds nest, and that the waters of this refuge swarm with all sorts of fresh-water fish and other creatures; thus the available food supply was unlimited, and that used was undoubtedly the easiest to procure.

The following record of three nestings of alligators at Avery Island, Louisiana are interesting:

First, because the actual record of incubation period.

Second, because of actual measurements of the eggs and of the newly-hatched young.

Third, because of the record of the length and weight of the mothers of each nest.

NEST No. 1:
Eggs laid June 21, 1921.
Eggs hatched August 22.
Incubation period 63 days.
Number of eggs, 42.
Average length of eggs 2.71 inches.
    "   width of eggs 1.67 inch.
    "   weight of eggs 3 1/16 ounces.
    "   length of young 9.41 inches.
Length of mother 9 ft., 1½ inches.
Weight of mother 163½ lbs.

NEST No. 2:
Eggs laid June 23, 1931.
Eggs hatched August 28.
Incubation period 67 days.
Number of eggs, 34.

Average length of eggs 2.61 inches.
"   width of eggs 1.60 inch.
"   weight of eggs 2⅛ ounces.
"   length of ten young 8.75 inches.
"   weight of ten young 1.75 ounces.
Length of mother 7 ft., 3 inches.
Weight of mother 116½ pounds.

NEST No. 3:
Eggs laid June 2, 1933.
Eggs hatched August 7.
Incubation period 66 days.
Number of eggs, 41.
Average length of eggs 2.63 inches.
"   width of eggs 1.61 inch.
"   weight of eggs 2¼ ounces.
"   length of young 9.19 inches.
"   weight of young 1 15/16 ounce.
Length of mother 7 ft., 8 inches.
Weight of mother 129½ pounds.

That the alligator has already been exterminated over a large portion of its former habitat is a fact, and one that civilization should not be proud of. There is, and will be for many years to come, a few spots in our swamps and marshes difficult of access to man, in which a few alligators will survive long enough to reach the reproducing age, so the actual total extermination of these harmless and picturesque reptiles is not an immediate danger; but it is extremely doubtful if they ever again will be an attractive feature of our waterways, as they were during the latter part of the last century.

In order to give alligators an opportunity to develop naturally and without fear of being molested, I have set aside about five thousand acres of lowland, suited to their needs, lying east and north of Avery Island in which no alligators are to be killed. This land is so protected by barriers that it is not easy of access; yet, during the past

Summer three different parties of alligator hunters were caught with head-lights and guns killing the alligators for their hides in the protected area, and it seems as if I will have to maintain a constant patrol of this area at night, if full protection is to be given them. This refuge was closed to all hunting three years ago, and already there has been a very large increase in the number of small alligators, but it will requite ten years more of protection before they will be sufficiently large to be a real feature of the waterways. Let us hope this protection can be given them.